Vasily Sesemann
Selected Papers

On the Boundary of Two Worlds: Identity, Freedom, and Moral Imagination in the Baltics

21

Editor

Leonidas Donskis, Member of the European Parliament, and previously Professor and Dean of Vytautas Magnus University School of Political Science and Diplomacy in Kaunas, Lithuania.

Editorial and Advisory Board

Timo Airaksinen, University of Helsinki, Finland
Egidijus Aleksandravicius, Lithuanian Emigration Institute, Vytautas Magnus University, Kaunas, Lithuania
Stefano Bianchini, University of Bologna, Forlì Campus, Italy
Endre Bojtar, Institute of Literary Studies, Budapest, Hungary
Kristian Gerner, University of Lund, Sweden
John Hiden, University of Glasgow, UK
Martyn Housden, University of Bradford, UK
Mikko Lagerspetz, Åbo Academy, Finland
Andreas Lawaty, Nordost-Institute, Lüneburg, Germany
Olli Loukola, University of Helsinki, Finland
Hannu Niemi, University of Helsinki, Finland
Alvydas Nikzentaitis, Lithuanian History Institute, Lithuania
Yves Plasseraud, Paris, France
Rein Raud, Rector of Tallinn University, Estonia
Alfred Erich Senn, University of Wisconsin-Madison, USA, and Vytautas Magnus University, Kaunas, Lithuania
David Smith, University of Glasgow, UK
Saulius Suziedelis, Millersville University, USA
Joachim Tauber, Nordost-Institut, Lüneburg, Germany
Tomas Venclova, Yale University, USA

Vasily Sesemann
Selected Papers

Translated from Lithuanian by
Mykolas Drunga

Edited by
Mykolas Drunga and Leonidas Donskis

Introduced by
Arūnas Sverdiolas

Amsterdam - New York, NY 2010

© Cover photo: "Vyborg", by Eeli Aalto

The paper on which this book is printed meets the requirements of "ISO 9706:1994, Information and documentation - Paper for documents - Requirements for permanence".

ISBN: 978-90-420-2825-8
E-Book ISBN: 978-90-420-2826-5
© Editions Rodopi B.V., Amsterdam - New York, NY 2010
Printed in the Netherlands

M. K. Čiurlionis. Sonata of the Stars. Andante. 1908

M. K. Čiurlionis National Art Museum
Photograph by Arūnas Baltėnas

Contents

Acknowledgements vii

Editors' Preface: Sighting and Sizing Up Sesemann . . . ix

Vasily Sesemann: The Other and Time,
   by Arūnas Sverdiolas xv

1. Aesthetic Evaluation in the History of Art
   (On the Relation between Art History and Aesthetics) . . 1

2. Aesthetics 29

3. Aesthetic Culture and Aesthetic Education 33

4. Physical Education and Aesthetic Culture 39

5. Protecting the Culture and the Beauty of the Past . . . 45

6. The Issue of National Culture 49

7. New Directions in Contemporary Epistemology 55

8. A Review of Worobiow's Book on Čiurlionis 81

Acknowledgements

This volume continues the Finnish-Lithuanian academic liaison that began with the publication, in this series, of a translation of Vasily Sesemann's *Aesthetics* into English. First and foremost, therefore, our thanks go to Dr. Olli Loukola, Professor of Social and Moral Philosophy at the University of Helsinki. It was primarily his encouragement, enthusiasm, and financial support that made it possible to publish this English-language version of Sesemann's papers. In this rediscovery of Sesemann as a scholarly nexus between Finland and Lithuania, the engagement of Dr. Hannu Niemi, Dean of the Social Science Faculty of the University of Helsinki and Professor of Statistics, was crucially important.

Since many of these papers appeared as appendices to the Lithuanian edition (1970) of Sesemann's *Aesthetics*, our thanks are due to its editor Dr. Albinas Lozuraitis and to the Mintis Publishing Co. (Vilnius, Lithuania) for allowing us to publish them in English with Editions Rodopi B.V. Dr. Lozuraitis and Mintis also deserve our gratitude for permission to include a paper from a 1987 collection of Sesemann's works.

Still other papers appeared in a Lithuanian-language collection published in 1997. We therefore thank its editor Dr. Loreta Anilionytė as well as Mintis Publishing Co. for permission to translate and publish them.

We also express our gratitude to the M. K. Čiurlionis National Art Museum and its director Mr. Osvaldas Daugelis for permission to publish reproductions of two of Čiurlionis's paintings.

Finally, we thank Mr. Saulius Bajorinas for helping with the design and preparing the page layout.

Mykolas Drunga
Leonidas Donskis
September 2009

Editors' Preface:
Sighting and Sizing Up Sesemann

What can the reader expect to find in this volume? What is missing from it that might have been included? And why is Vasily Sesemann important? Let's start by looking at the latter question from the widest perspective.

In the context of European philosophy, Vasily Sesemann (1884–1963) might indeed seem be the somewhat *marginal* philosopher that Arūnas Sverdiolas takes him to be in his Introduction to this book. But even if this is correct, it is far from making him slight and unimportant.

For consider: if European philosophy is thought of as centered in Germany, Austria, and France, as is often the case in so-called Continental academic reflections, then even Britain ends up a bit off the beaten track, not to mention Italy and Spain and most of the rest of Europe (in all directions). But move the center just a little *east* or *northeast* of Germany, that is, move it to what actually *used to be* northeasternmost Germany—to Königsberg, for example, where the greatest of all German philosophers spent his entire life, or to Riga, where one of his greatest books was first published, or to both, where one of his greatest students not only influenced the 19th-century national revivals of Eastern European peoples but also foundationally contributed to classical interpretative scholarship; hermeneutics; linguistics; anthropology; and modern history and philosophy of culture, thought, and language—and an entirely new perspective opens up. Then the "marginal" Sesemann ends up right in the middle of what might be called German-Polish-Baltic-Nordic-Russian philosophy; and in that context he is far from marginal but rather a worthy pupil of Kant and Herder.

Of course, in this (by no means homogeneous) philosophical concatenation it is the German component that bears the most intellectual weight. Moreover, this bloc (call it *Nordic*) is on the whole less significant than another one (call it *Western*) that might also be concatenated, starting again with Germany but now looking northwestward, westward, and southwestward, to form (the no less heterogeneous) German-French-British-Italian-Spanish philosophy. The Nordic bloc is indeed less illustrious than the Western one; but this is in part for reasons having to do not so much with the quality of the philosophy originally created there as with the political circumstances under which particularly the eastern portions of this Nordic bloc had to live for large stretches of the last two or three centuries. Hand-in-hand with the relatively miserable political conditions went a lack of access to venues where European culture in general was publicized, promoted, and discussed.

Thus, for example, Polish logic was able not only to come into existence and flower but also to earn recognition as a major contribution to world intellectual culture when and only when Poland regained its national independence after World War I and the free movement of East European people and ideas became (at least for a while) a reality.

Similarly (though admittedly on a smaller scale in comparison to Polish philosophy) Vasily Sesemann would be much better known in the world today if like Nicolai Hartmann, his friend from St. Petersburg, he had written and published his major works in German (and Germany) rather than in Lithuanian (and Lithuania). That he favored the latter turned out to be a great boon to it—Lithuania received a first-rate scholar in the fields of aesthetics, epistemology, logic, and history of philosophy.

On the other hand, the fact that Sesemann taught and published in the "boondocks" is (to repeat) in part why his relative importance is still not widely appreciated. Another reason why he is less celebrated than, for example, Hartmann lies in the fact that although the former's *Aesthetics* is probably equal in value to any single work written by the latter, Sesemann did not construct an original system of his own but contented himself with just fairly, judiciously, and thoroughly expounding (and questioning) the philosophical ideas of others, both modern and ancient. Although for nearly two decades he taught philosophy at the University of Lithuania in Kaunas, he was neither the founder nor a follower of any philosophical school—just a brilliant and critical teacher who (together with the Swiss-educated Stasys Šalkauskis) helped raise a whole generation of Lithuanian philosophers later active not only in Lithuania but also, and indeed predominantly so, in the West.

It was Lithuania's tragedy to be occupied by, and completely lose political independence and be annexed to, the Soviet Union in 1940 and again in 1944. Lithuania, as a "constituent republic" of the SSSR, did not even have a shadow of the formal token independence that Poland and the other Warsaw Pact nations enjoyed until the dissolution of the Iron Curtain in the late 1980s and the Soviet Union's breakup in the early 1990s, which latter developments helped secure whatever in the way of a safer kind of sovereignty Lithuania (and, for that matter, the whole of Eastern Europe southward from Finland) at present still has. For Sesemann himself, this Lithuanian tragedy played itself out in the fact that he spent six years in a Soviet forced-labor camp, for which reason his work was only sparsely published as long as the Soviets were in power.

In this context it becomes understandable why Sesemann is so late in arriving on the scene of Western European intellectual consciousness. The first work of his translated from the Lithuanian and published in the West is the above-mentioned *Aesthetics* (Rodopi: Amsterdam, New York,

2007). The second is this volume of Selected Papers. It contains translations into English of some noteworthy essays, ranging from the scholarly to the popular, on aesthetics, aesthetic education, national culture, and theory of knowledge—all fields that Sesemann cared deeply about and enriched.

Nevertheless, it contains by no means everything that he wrote in the Lithuanian language and/or that was published in Lithuania (and which is therefore difficult to access by a non-Lithuanian reader). For one, it does not contain (with one exception) the many valuable articles on philosophical topics that he wrote for the *Lietuviškoji enciklopedija* [Lithuanian Encyclopedia], which began to be published in 1931 and was discontinued in 1944 (after 8 volumes up to the letter *J*) because of the occupation. The list of these encyclopedia articles is impressive: it includes (but is not limited to) entries on *Anaxagoras*; *Anaximander*; *Antisthenes*; *Aristotle*; *atheism*; *Bacon,* Francis; *Bergson,* Henri; *Byzantine philosophy*; *Comte,* Auguste; *Croce,* Benedetto; *deduction*; *definition*; *dialectics*; *empiricism*; *Epicurus*; *Epictetus*; *Fechner,* Gustav Theodor; *phenomenon*; *phenomenology*; *Feuerbach,* Ludwig; *Fichte,* Johann Gottlieb; *gnosticism*; *Gorgias*; *Greek philosophy*; *Guyau,* Jean Marie; *Hartmann,* Eduard; *Hartmann,* Nikolai; *hedonism*; *Hegel,* G. F. W.; *Hegelianism*; *Heidegger,* Martin; *Helvetius,* Claude Adrien; *Heraclitus*; *Herder,* Johann Gottfried; *Hobbes,* Thomas; *Holbach,* Paul; *Husserl,* Edmund; *I* (ego), *idea*; *idealism*; *infinity, space*.

Since publication of the encyclopedia was forcibly stopped just before the letter *J*, one can only imagine how many more such articles Sesemann would have produced had he been given the chance. Those listed here possess a quality which would bring honor to any American, British, French, or German encyclopedia. They are clear and sober introductions, never oversimplified, to the topic at hand; especially weighty and detailed are the entries on Aristotle, Fichte, Greek philosophy, phenomenon, phenomenology, Hegel, Herder, Husserl, idealism, and space (in Lithuanian, *erdvė*). The main reason we have not included translations of them in this volume is that unfortunately that would take up too much space.

But there is one exception: we have included the encyclopedia article "Aesthetics" because it is an early and succinct survey of one of Sesemann's main areas of specialization, a field in which he published heavily. While his already alluded-to *Aesthetics* textbook (which contains reflections and investigations carried out as late as the 1950s) was one of the few books by him published posthumously in Soviet times, the papers collected here, including the encyclopedia article, were all composed in the 1920s and 1930s.

Thus "Aesthetic Evaluation in the History of Art: On the Relation Between Art History and Aesthetics" was originally written in Russian and published in the journal *Mysl'* (Petrograd: 1922, Nr. 1, p. 117–147), and much later translated into Lithuanian by Juozas Tumelis. This Lithuanian version, from which the essay in the present volume was translated, was published, along with other papers on aesthetics, in the collection *Estetika* (Vilnius, 1970), of which the just-mentioned textbook constituted the bulk.

Not included in the present volume is an equally valuable essay, "On the Nature of the Poetic Image," reprinted in the 1970 collection and, again, originally written in Russian but first published in the Proceedings of the University of Lithuania Humanities Faculty (*Lietuvos universiteto humanitarinių mokslų fakulteto raštai*, Book One, Kaunas, 1925, p. 423–481). However, a much abbreviated version of this essay already appeared in English as Appendix II of Thorsten Botz-Bornstein's study *Vasily Sesemann: Experience, Formalism, and the Question of Being* (Rodopi: Amsterdam, New York, 2006), which is a useful guide, *inter alia*, to some of the literary and philological aspects of Sesemann's thought.

Another early paper on aesthetics, but now written in Lithuanian and not as explicitly scholarly, is included in this volume: "Aesthetic Culture and Aesthetic Education," first published in *Vairas* (1924, No. 8, p. 10–12) and republished in the 1970 collection, from which it was translated here.

Sesemann was much interested in body culture and physical education, as evidenced by his 1935 article on "Physical Education and Aesthetic Culture," first printed in *Fiziškas auklėjimas* (1935, No. 2, p. 3–8) and here translated from the 1970 collection.

The physical culture not of the human body but of man-made objects is the topic of the essay, "Protecting the Culture and the Beauty of the Past," first published in *Naujoji Romuva* (1938, No. 22–24, p. 511–512) and again translated here from its version in the 1970 collection.

"The Issue of National Culture" first appeared in the *Akademikas* student magazine (Kaunas, 1934, Nr. 15(32), p. 342–344). Here it was translated from its reprinting in the volume *Vosylius Sezemanas. Raštai. Filosofijos istorija, Kultūra* (Vilnius: Mintis 1997).

This article contains one of several passages in his works where Sesemann discusses Mikalojus Konstantinas Čiurlionis (1875–1911), the curiously original Lithuanian painter and composer who probably would have become much more famous than in fact he was had he exhibited in Munich rather than St. Petersburg. This is not a claim that Sesemann makes (though we do); but what Sesemann does emphasize is that Čiurlionis embodies the national spirit in a way neither superficial nor showy nor exclusive yet still universal and at the same time unique. It is evident that the points Sesemann makes about Lithuanian national culture can be carried over, *mutatis mutandis*, to other cultures as well.

Čiurlionis's art is the main topic of Sesemann's review of a monograph by the art historian Nikolaj Worobiow. The review first appeared in *Naujoji Romuva* (1938, No. 49). Here it is translated once more from the 1970 collection. The editors of this volume thought that in view of the importance both of Čiurlionis and of Sesemann's valuation of him it is entirely fitting that this book be illustrated with some characteristic reproductions of the Lithuanian painter-musician's work.

Finally, it is crucial to realize that Sesemann's interests embraced not only practical philosophy but theoretical philosophy as well, of which logic and epistemology were the most important.

In Kaunas he published his university lectures on logic in Lithuanian as *Logika* (1929) as well as some substantial studies in German, including "Die logischen Gesetze und das Sein: a) Die logischen Gesetze im Verhältnis zum subjektbezogenen und psychischen Sein. b) Die logischen Gesetze und das daseinsautonome Sein" in *Eranus*, Vol. 2 (Kaunas: 1931; 60–230) and "Zum Problem der logischen Paradoxien" in *Eranus*, Vol. 3 (Kaunas: 1935; 5–85). None of these have been translated here.

Even more weighty were Sesemann's writings on epistemology, most of which were also published in pre-war Kaunas, although some were written in German and only posthumously translated into Lithuanian. His essays on objectual and non-objectual knowledge, on rationality and irrationality, and on logical rationality have not been translated into English for this volume, as they would take up a separate volume by themselves. But they are available in Lithuanian in his *Raštai. Gnoseologija* (Vilnius: Mintis, 1987).

Originally written in Lithuanian (and published in Kaunas) was a series of university lectures on the topic titled *Gnoseologija* and comparable to the *Logika* mentioned above. That, too, has not been translated here. But there is one important epistemological essay (originally published in *Eranus*, Vol. 3, 1935) whose translation into English we have decided to include. That is his explorations of "New Directions in Contemporary Epistemology"; this lively study is significant for its views on thought's dynamism and its anticipations of, and harmonizing with, process philosophy.

Sesemann's appreciation of, and fascination with, change is evident in another important essay, "Time, Culture, and Body: Getting to Know the Challenges of Contemporary Culture." Since this work is discussed in great detail in Sverdiolas's Preface, we have not undertaken to translate it for this volume, although arguaby we should have.

There is even more—much more—in Sesemann's *oeuvre* that has not been translated into English. Many of these texts are in the already referred-to Lithuanian collection *Raštai. Filosofijos istorija, Kultūra* (Vilnius: Mintis 1997). They concern ancient Greek philosophy and later history of philosophy, especially German, at least up to existentialism;

there are also lectures on toleration, the problem of freedom, the problem of suffering, the problem of the bourgeoisie, Christianity and socialism, the ideological significance of religion as well as sundry book reviews.

Another segment of Sesemann's output that awaits translation into English consists of his Russian writings. The existence and importance of these is poignant in view of the circumstance (reported by Botz-Bornstein on p. 14 of his aforementioned book) that Sesemann's Eurasian inclinations might have caused him to be sent to the Gulag; in any case this Russian angle once again underscores the fact that Sesemann was a proverbial Nordic philosophical bridge bwetween East and West.

All in all, it seems that Sesemann truly was a prolific writer; the editors of the aforesaid collection indicate that there is enough material (published but for the most part unpublished) left behind for several more Lithuanian-language collections at least.

If this is so, then Vasily Sesemann's "return to (Western) Europe" is not that far behind his return to Lithuania, his adopted land, itself.

Mykolas Drunga
Leonidas Donskis

VASILY SESEMANN: THE OTHER AND TIME

Arūnas Sverdiolas

Vasily Sesemann: A Contemporary Philosopher?

In some respects, Vasily Sesemann is a uniquely contemporary figure. His biography, his work, and his historical fate all exhibit an unbreakable connection of the global and the local; they merge a universality of horizons with a particularity of trajectories. His identity as a person and as a thinker crystallized in several markedly distinct cultural and linguistic contexts without completely fitting into any one of them. Sesemann was both at home in, and alien to, a number of cultural traditions to which, at one or another period of his life, he was intimately related. He wrote philosophical works in Russian, German, and Lithuanian; and he wrote personal letters in these languages and Swedish, too. His Russian texts, however, were published mainly in the émigré press, which was unavailable and forbidden in Soviet Russia; his German texts appeared mostly in scholarly journals; and his Lithuanian writings became part of a small literary heritage largely unknown to the rest of the world. In this way Sesemann was and remained a marginal polymorph, so to speak. Those wishing to discern all sides of him need to follow him through terrains that changed in more ways than merely language. Nevertheless, his philosophical output accorded well with the basic dynamism of the philosophical thought of his times; it interacted with some of the most important philosophical currents and constituted an individual variety thereof.

Sesemann was born on May 30 (June 6), 1884 in Vyborg (on what was then Finnish territory) into the family of a Swedish father and a German mother. His childhood and youth were spent in a Russian cultural milieu in St. Petersburg. From 1903 to 1909 he attended St. Petersburg University, where he studied philosophy with the Russian intuitionist Nikolai Lossky and classical philology with the Polish professor Tadeusz Zielinski. Then he went to Marburg and Berlin to pursue further philosophical studies with the neo-Kantians Hermann Cohen, Paul Natorp, and Ernst Cassirer; he also studied art history with Heinrich Wölfflin. Upon his return to Russia he taught for a few years in St. Petersburg and had his writings published in German periodicals and in the Russian *Logos*.

After World War I Sesemann continued teaching for a while in Russia but soon left for Berlin where he was associated with Russian émigré publishing houses and scholarly institutions. In 1923 he was invited to teach at the newly established University of Lithuania in Kaunas, became a professor there, and together with the university moved to Vilnius in 1940. In 1950 he was arrested and spent six years in the Gulag. After being released he was allowed to work as professor of logic until his death on March 23, 1963 in Vilnius. Thus he spent a large part of his life in Lithuania; there he wrote his most mature works and taught the longest. He learned the language perfectly; contributed to the development of Lithuanian philosophical terminology; and translated Aristotle's *De Anima* into Lithuanian.

Sesemann's work has been taken note of in all the cultural communities in which he lived, but up to now this was mostly in Lithuania.[1] Slowly his ouevre is being published, with many translations from the Russian and German languages; his books *Logika* and *Estetika* have come out; and journals have re-published his articles and published his letters. His works have drawn the attention of historians of philosophy. Those of his manuscripts that have not been printed are preserved in the Vilnius University Library and the National Martynas Mažvydas Library. Once Lithuania regained independence accounts of hitherto blacked-out episodes in his biography—the persecution he had to endure up to, including, and after his Gulag incarceration—have become public. Many people hold his memory in reverence. He arouses interest in Finland. Several reprints of his texts appeared in Russia. The first more ambitious attempts to present Sesemann to international philosophical audiences are a monograph written by Thorsten Botz-Bornstein,[2] indispensable to anyone who wishes to delve into Sesemann's philosophy more deeply, and a translation of his *Aesthetics* by Mykolas Drunga.[3] The present collection of essays will substantially extend our acquaintance with this unique thinker.

Historians of philosophy have observed that Sesemann's philosophical road was a movement away from a Marburgian Neo-Kantianism toward a rather ill-defined and heterogeneous complex of thoughts characterized as critical realism or ontological problematics.[4] He is also associated with Russian intuitionist philosophy, first of all that of his teacher Nikolai Lossky. These confluences determine the nature of Sesemann's thinking. He did not develop an autonomous philosophical language but made use of idiomatics borrowed from several sources; he thought them through in seeking a path of his own, making them more precise or sometimes criticizing one of them with the help of another. He was sensitive to truly new and valuable things and rendered independent judgment on them: when Martin Heidegger's *Sein und Zeit* appeared, he immediately noticed it and wrote a review in which he forthrightly declared: "this is a splendid book; undoubtedly the finest to appear in the last 10 or 15 years; in terms of originality and depth it is comparable only to the best works of Max Scheler."[5] We should remember that at that time Scheler was much better-known and a much greater authority than Heidegger. Sesemann also took note of and correctly appraised the novelty of Ludwig Wittgenstein's *Philosophical Investigations*, which had just appeared.[6]

Though dynamically changing, Sesemann's work nevertheless preseved a certain unified direction and core. He continuously attempted to overcome an unreflected-on fundamental presupposition of modern philosophy, the opposition of subject and object. Driven by this quest, his philosophical thought transformed itself from Russian Intuitionism and partly Marburgian Kantianism into something approaching philosophy of life (*Lebensphilosophie*) and especially phenomenology, though without fully identyifying with either. In the dynamic complex of his ideas ontological problematics always predominated, analyzed from the point of view of so-called nonobjectual (non-thing-related) cognition.

He distinguished an objectifying and objectual knowing (*gegenständliches Wissen*), which he analyzed mostly on the level of logic: he investigated the time of logic, associating it with the past, as well as the nature of logical patadoxes. This knowing is not something spontaneous and elemental; it is based on a peculiar attitude of consciousness going about its special task of objectifying (*Vergegenständlichung*), which is making reality into an object. But this objectual thinking does not grasp reality itself: logic is the logic not of being itself but of an objectified being subordinated to cognition. So what is reality itself grasped by? The objectifying mode of consciousness is not the only one. There is also another, non-objectifying and non-objectual knowing (*ungegenständliches Wissen*), to the articulation of which Sesemann devoted most of his efforts.

This is a peculiarly practical, signification-rich, and value-laden cognition or, more exactly, experience, envisaging an immediate and essential participation of the subject in the multi-faceted reality perceived by him. For instance, the presence of mental phenomena to consciousness is not objectual. Here Sesemann appealed to the psychology of his times, especially that of Theodor Lipps; he also dealt with the problematics of experience in Wilhem Dilthey's so-called descriptive psychology. Mental being is pre-objective; i.e., it is more fundamental than the logical definitions of being.

However, non-objectual cognition is not limited to mental phenomena; it embraces the phenomena of so-called spiritual being or culture: history, ethics, religion, meanings, and values.

Sesemann paid particular attention to aesthetics. This reality cannot be adequately investigated through concepts and is grasped only through acts of direct empathy (*Einfühlung*) or perception tied to concrete, individual experience. This kind of experience may be called cognition only in a very conditional sense. But intuitionism also does not appear to Sesemann to be a suitable method of thinking; he talks about a special kind of self-reflection, and moves towards phenomenology and hermeneutics. Thus, in his detailed analyses of the experience of art, time, or whatever, the center of attention is occupied each time by a different attitude and by the proper givenness of this or that phenomenon. The essential features of this experience come to the fore during a special act of self-reflexion, when it is not the case that the object of cognition is transcendent in relation to the subject (if it is still possible to apply these concepts here) but rather the multifaceted reality concretely and fully discloses itself to the subject. It is this being of consciousness, revealing itself to self-reflexion, that must become the true object of philosophical thought. Experience understood and reflected this way blossoms out in the horizon of post-Nietzschean thought, a horizon common to philosophy of life, phenomenology, and hermeneutics.

The philosophical and historical analysis of Sesemann's ideas evidently will continue as their segments, stages, and contexts are clarified in greater detail. Our own restrospective glance recognizes that the directions taken by philosophical thought at that time flourish in an already demarcated mental territory; thus the movement of Sesemann's thought can be precisely located among these tendencies and recognized as such. This was not yet the case in his own time, when these directional lines and borders were still being sketched, and he was moving with them and marking out his own lines.

But the historical approach is not the only one worth applying to Sesemann's ideas. An analytical and constructive approach is also possible. Then one would not be placing one or the other philosophical conception of his in the context of the philosophy of his period, but would be looking at it in the perspective of future philosophy or philosophy in general, seeking to uncover its inner logic and its potential for presently relevant thought. To do this systematically is a task for the future. Prior to this one must discuss the various thematic levels.

One thing worth looking for in Sesemann's philosophy is an attempt to reflect on the relations between the Other and time. To be sure, Sesemann did not discuss the Other explicitly; in his texts this concept is not used very systematically, although it does appear in rather significant contexts. Thus, in his analyses of problems related to time, to which he devoted considerable attention, we do hit upon the problem of the Other and Otherness. Self-perception is a never-ending task; both its essential boundary and its essential condition is the inner time of consciousness, constantly creating the non-identity of consciousness with itself and disallowing an unlimited going back to the same thing. Analyzing the time of consciousness, Sesemann discovers the beginnings of the problematics of the fracturing of identity and of it as the Other.

The deep connections between the problematic of the Other and that of time characterize not only Sesemann's philosophy but philosophy in general. Help in looking for and actualizing these connections may be found in the work of Emmanuel Lévinas—incidentally, another thinker with ties to Lithuania. His analysis can serve as a contrasting background for highlighting the appropriate ideas of Sesemann. The common arena enabling a fruitful comparison of their ideas is phenomenology. To be sure, neither one nor the other may be called a phenomenologist without essential qualification and explanation, and the relationship of each to phenomenology was different. However, a certain kind of analysis allows us to state that Sesemann philosophized at the border of pre-phenomenology and phenomenology, whereas Lévinas philosophized at the border of phenomenology and post-phenomenology, and that both philosophers often transgressed these boundaries, albeit in opposite directions. Yet it is just for this reason that it makes sense to compare these two thinkers, since the issue of phenomenology's boundaries remains live today, something that cannot be said about, for example, the vicissitudes of late neo-Kantianism, which are interesting only to historians of philosophy.[7]

The rudiments of both the problematics of the Other and that of time have been present in the most ancient thought from Parmenides onwards up to the German idealism of Johann Gottlieb Fichte and Georg Wilhem Friedrich Hegel. But the modern discussion on the level of polycentric egology began only in the 20th century. It was then that the so-called philosophy of dialogue championed the requirement that the Other be considered first of all as another person, as a partner in an existence-defining dialogue. Martin Buber connected the *thou* (*Du*) with a special relationship to human beings, a relationship essentially different from the theoretical cognitive or pragmatic relationship to a thing (and to a human as a thing) conceived as an anonymous *it* (*es*). The problem of the Other began to worry phenomenology as soon as it turned its attention to the problematics of intersubjectivity. It was Edmund Husserl who had raised the question, How does the consciousness that constitutes the universe of meanings, the transcendental *I* relate to another *I*, the *alter ego*? When Jean-Paul Sartre delved into this problem, the Other became important as someone looking at and perceiving me, thus constituting my very selfhood as a being-for-another. Alternately put, the existence of the *I* can realize itself only through an Other, in relation to an Other. This, according to Sartre, is equally applicable to the Other, so that the I and the Other are in this respect symmetrical, reciprocal. The Hermeneutic philosophy of Wilhelm Dilthey and Hans-Georg Gadamer raised the question of the Other at the level of a peculiarly conceived time, of an always newly begun dialogue with a tradition growing steadily more alien. Finally, the problematics of the Other is peculiarly significant to poststructuralism; it appears in a new guise in postmodern thinking.

But perhaps the most radical approach to the problematics of the Other is that of Lévinas, who held all earlier attempts to analyze it as inadequate. One of the most important thematic levels at which Lévinas discusses the Other is that of time. Classical and modern philosophy treated time either as objective time standing in a wholly external relation to the subject or as subjective time wholly internal to the transcendental subject. Concerning the latter, the purest expression of which is probably found in Kant, Lévinas observes, looking at it from his own angle: "The utterly single *I*, the monad, already had a time."[8] Such an undiscussed but presupposed monoegologicality is also characteristic of the most important modern thinkers about time—Henri Bergson and Martin Heidegger. Lévinas, however, quite categorically states that "to us, it appears impossible to speak of the lonely subject's time, of a purely personal duration."[9] In the very first sentence of his book *Time and the Other* he states his goal thus: "to show that time is not a fact about an isolated and lonely subject but is that subject's very relation to another person."[10] Thus the problems of time and the Other are most intimately tied together.

So we have a context in which not objectual but also subjective (or more precisely, monoobjective) time is critiqued; and we have a background in which the essential connection of the time of human existence with the Other, with the interpersonal relation is asserted. It is in this context and against this background that Sesemann's endeavor to think though the relations between the Other and time stands out in relief and may be understood more correctly. But first we must take a look at some general features of Sesemann's analysis of time.

Logical and Existential Time

Sesemann was concerned not only with one aspect of Time; he discussed it on several very different levels. He called attention to it in his gnoseological studies where he asked, What sort of Time is presupposed by logic? This question may seem unexpected, since it is usually thought that logical structures are simply atemporal, that they have no relation to Time. But the question about the time of logic is connected with the question about the very core of logic, its identity; it makes a problem out of this core by asking about its relationship with the Other. Now the level of logic is secured by the *law of identity*: a is a.[11] In other words, logical time is the time of identity; here, we might say, is just the selfsame thing and no otherness appears. But Sesemann observes that a judgment already harbors nonidentity, novelty, dynamism. Like Hegel, he speaks of the movement of concepts within the judgment and argument.

Nonetheless this dialectical dynamism of logical time did not suffice for Sesemann; he tried to grap time's dynamism phenomenologically. As already discussed, he was concerned with experience, an area much broader than that of logical judgment and argument. It is in this preobjectual being that the topic of experience's peculiar time arises. We will get to this presently. But even if it is analyzed in its dynamical aspect, logical time essentially differs from real time in lacking duration. Crucially, logical eternity is not actual.[12] Yet philosophy at the very least since Aristotle very clearly seeks to reflect on actuality because only actual being is being in the true sense of that word. Furthermore, the "difference between past, present, and future is totally alien to the time of logic."[13] But past, present, and future are just the essential, irreducible varieties of experiential or existential time.

In modern Western philosophy the topic of Becoming and Time is constantly expanding and deepening; as Sesemann states, it "encompasses all of the reality accessible to humans"[14] and demands a special kind of reflection. One may say that after Hegel and Nietzsche the conception of universal and all-embracing Time becomes the horizon of philosophical thinking, at teast the declared horizon. It is in this horizon that Sesemann also aims to reflect. I say "declared" and "aims" because it is a very difficult task for the execution of which it is not enough just to declare a program. No wonder Nietzsche's call to vanquish Platonism is so often repeated today: it is much easier to declare it and to assent to it than to realize it consistently in one's thinking practice. Sesemann, by the way, in 1923 raised a contrary call—that of reviving Platonism.[15]

He is most interested in experiential or existential Time, the conception of which had been expounded by Saint Augustine in a way decisive for most of the further tradition of Western thought. To be sure, Sesemann does not mention Augustine in connection with the problematics of Time, and only formally mentions him in connection with the problematics of self-reflection. But that doesn't matter; Sesemann takes from the tradition the fundamental features of the conception of time, and these were articulated by Augustine. In his study *Time, Culuture, and Body: Getting to Know the Challenges of Contemporary Culture*, published in Lithuanian as *Laikas, kultūra ir kūnas. Šių dienų kultūros uždaviniams pažinti* in 1933,[16] Sesemann emphasizes that the flow of time is unstoppable, unique, and irreversible: "The past never comes back and cannot again become the present. Each moment, every situation is the one and only one of its kind and therefore cannot be repeated."[17] He also calls attention to the fundamentally destructive feature of Time: "by dividing being into the past, the present, and the future, it simultaneously destroys the reality of being."[18] This property, called attention to by Augustine, frequently crops up, even if only non-thematically, in reflections on experiential and existential Time. An analysis of the experience of time reveals that "true reality, it seems, is only the present; it is only through its mediation that the past and the future partake in reality. The past is real only because it was the present. The future is real only insofar as it will become the present."[19]

Besides Augustine, we should also recall Heidegger, whose ideas Sesemann regarded highly, especially his phenomenological analysis of the elemental and all-embracing temporality of existence. This is how he expounds Heidegger's thought: "The past here signifies not what no longer is, what was in the past. And the future signifies not what isn't there yet but will be there later. To understand the temporality of anxiety in this way is to equate anxiety's being with the being of things, that is, with a being coinciding with [a thing's] givenness [наличие, Heidegger's *Vorhandene—A.S.*]. [...] The temporal existence of Being-consciousness [бытие–сознание; this is how Sesemann rendered Heidegger's *Dasein* in Russian and Lithuanian[20]] is not Being in time, a Being that presupposes temporality; rather it is a Being in concert with which temporality is born and constitutes itself."[21] Heidegger's anxiety, with which temporality is associated, is in a way an analogue of Husserl's reduction: they both have to make sure that philosophical analysis concern itself not with objectual and objective being, but with the being of consciousness, being here and now or conscious being (one more synonym used by Sesemann[22]); that is, the most important object of philosophical reflection.

Sesemann attempts to reconcile Augustine's and Heidegger's conceptions of time. Furthermore, what he describes as the special reality and actuality of the present may also be understood as self-identity: essentially one's own is only that which is now. The deep fracture of time asserted by Sesemann affects the distribution of self-identity and, respectively, otherness along the axis of time: we might say that only the present appears to belong to one's self, whereas the past and the future appear to belong to the other, even the alien—and this in two (and rather different) ways.

Similarly important is another Augustinian thesis of Sesemann's, namely, that the present moment is forever disappearing: "the direct reality of the present moment cannot be caught. When we say 'this is', then this already was and thereby has become past and ceased to be present. And to the extent this has has not yet happened, but is in the process of happening, this is in the future and is conditional on, and given meaning by, future moments; consequently, it isn't yet there as as a reality. In this way the reality of the present vanishes. It appears it is nothing other than an ideal limit, an extensionless point, a moment without duration, in which an unreal future passes into an equally unreal past."[23] We might add that this dialectic of vanishing characterizes ownness as well: ownness, too, cannot be caught between two varieties of temporal otherness, the past and the future.

Sesemann calls this experience of the vanishing of existence, made so apparent by the temporal level, "intolerable." It has to be radically overcome, since "its inevitable outcome is the destruction of life itself." That's why Sesemann sees it as task "to conquer time in time itself and to find in its non-being its true and real foundation. . . . It is in the qualities of time itself that we must seek and find such potentialities (possibilities) and forces as could not only arrest its destructive effect but also be used to create and manage life itself." But it is clear that neither the ceaselessness, nonrepeatability, and irreversibility of time's flow nor its fracturing into separate moments, into the varieties of past, present, and future can be simply done away with. These features of experiential time can only be transformed—by transforming experiece itself, existence itself. But how? Sesemann considers two different, we might say even opposed, strategies for overcoming the vanishing, the irreality, of time.

The time of culture and the otherness of time

Sesemann seeks the potential for a synthesis of the moments of fracturing time first of all in purposive action. "Every action or job performed *takes time*, i.e., it goes through a multitude of moments and therefore even as it is happening it embraces past, present, and future. . . Every action or job as it is going on conjoins past, present, and future into one meaningful whole in which not only the preceding moments ground and support those following but the latter as an envisioned continuation or goal (objective) condition and fashion the former."[24] Here Sesemann is stepping in the footsteps of Henri Bergson without mentioning him. The significant unity of purposive action conditions the transformation of time itself: it ties together past, present, and future into a unified happening in which they constrain one another. The reality of the three moments of time, including that of the present, depends on their relation to the totality of action encompassing all of them. Therefore "it is in meaningful action issuing in concrete results that the negativities of time acquire a positive value: time no longer destroys, but on the contrary, creates."[25]

For Sesemann purposive action has a direct relation with cultural activity. Reflection on this level of the philosophy of culture is connected not only with Bergson's analysis of duration but also with Heidegger's analysis of the elemental temporality of existence or even is directly founded on that analysis. It is especially important for Sesemann that true temporality reveals itself to a special attitude of consciousness or a special way of being, the so-called resoluteness.

"Resoluteness creates the self-hood of being-consciousness, envisaging and implementing its true possibilities. Such an envisaging and implementing is the *what-will-be* [*грядущее*]. It is what resoluteness is oriented towards; therefore in the order of authentic being it is accorded primacy."[26] On the other hand, in this orientation towards the future "there already lies a looking back to the authentic (ideal) past, as the voice of conscience testifies."[27]

Of course, the unity of three temporal moments that purposive action creates can only be dynamic and contradictory. Besides, in analyzing its dialectic Sesemann contents himself neither with Bergsonian duration nor Heideggerian envisaging but appeals to other conceptual tools taken over from 19th century German idealism and early 20th century philosophy of culture. These became foundational for Lithuanian philosophy of culture as well.[28] Purposive action is always directed by pursuit of results, which are always "objective goods or values which in any case remain even then when the activity that created them no longer goes on."[29] In this way the purposiveness of an action is identified with the pursuit of its result, which goes beyond the confines of the action itself. The Greeks held this to constitute the essence of *techne* and *poiesis*, the making of an artifact and the creation of an art work. To these might also be added *ethos*, behaviors, but only those having significant consequences; no such thing as a *beau geste*, playful activity for its own sake or Kantian activity purely out of respect for a principle would fit here.

In this way there unfolds the problematics of becoming a thing and ceasing to be one, of the relationship between subjective and objective culture, a problematics in which ownness and otherness interweave. Otherness (alterity) is the fundamental consideration in discussions about the alienation and being alien. By the way, in so-called primitive culture this dialectic of time and ownness as well as alienation supposedly do not exist: significant content or culture is "wholly actual, it wholly belongs to what is present."[30] From the point of view that now concerns us we might add that to a participant in a given culture that culture is wholly his or her own. But this state of it is only a seeming reference point chosen to throw light on the totally different nature of contemporary culture. To a human being living nowadays "such a state in which all his organic and spiritual forces would be wholly mobilized (actualized) at once is usually not attainable. Rather this mobilization itself becomes an act of culture (a job) that . . . has duration and happens in a certain order of separate moments."[31] Therefore contemporary existence is not concentrated in any single moment; it unfolds in three varieties of time. "Least of all does he [a man seeking a stable result of his action—*A.S.*] fit all in the now, the present. He proceeds from the past to the future, and the present means no more to him than the reality of the continuous connectedness of the future with the past."[32] What is now is conceived as one of the moments of purposive activity; it (the present) gets an auxiliary function that depends on both the past and the future. "He [the man acting in this way—*A.S.*] does not stop at the now, the present. This is just an intermediary point allowing the future to be tied with the past."[33]

It turns out that during the performance of a stable-result-seeking activity the moments of existential time are synthesized at the expense of the present, the now, the ownness—these are lost. Turning into a moment of a stable-result-seeking activity, the present, according to Sesemann, "has to lose its qualitative peculiarity, its special tension and vitality, . . . renounce its own specific (extraordinary) reality!"[34] Purposive activity not only is incapable of overcoming the vanishing of time, but also, we may say, it establishes and fortifies it.

Thus the strategy which I identified as the extension of the present and of ownness in all three variations of time, a strategy pursued in an effort to make them one's own, turns out to be unsuccessful. Indeed, the present being disintegrates, it gets lost in the varieties of time not made one's own; whereas ownness becomes alienated and turns into the other: moment after moment a man's existence becomes not his own because he himself is not his own, but is pro-jected in the etymological sense of the word, that is, he is "thrown forward" into the envisaged future of his activity and at the same time cast back to the past of collecting the resources subordinated to the project. Ownness appears as contaminated by the twofold otherness of time.

These negative conclusions are all the more important in that they contradict the thrust of Heidegger's views on temporality as described by Sesemann in the already-mentioned review. There he expounds Heidegger's thought as follows: "In authentic temporality the present does not stand out as an extraordinary moment alongside the past and the future. In the present what will be meets what has been; in other words, in resoluteness, actualizing itself in actions, what will be becomes the present of what has been (*Gewesenheit*)."[35]

In this context it makes sense to call forth the appropriate ideas of Lévinas. For he talks about the present and the future in a way similar to Sesemann, as if continuing the latter's thought to the end, to the limit; but then he resolutely steps beyond that limit and offers an alternative, which applies not only to Sesemann but to phenomenology in general. Lévinas, in contrast to Heidegger, believes that "future as envisioned, as projected . . . is only the future's present, not the real future. The future is what cannot be grasped, what falls over us and subjugates us. The future is the other."[36] Lévinas variously brings out what he calls the future's otherness (alterity), polemically contrasting it with Heidegger's analysis of existence as being-unto-death. For Heidegger death is important as an ineluctable though as a rule misunderstood horizon of all ways of existing, actions, and projects; thus it is an indirect, remaining-in-the-background anticipation. Meanwhile Lévinas emphasizes the incomparability of the future with any activity or project, its radical unownedness, ingraspability, its radical otherness. In the face of death a human being cannot undertake anything whatsoever; he can neither envisage it nor act towards it. Death is transcendence, radical otherness, independent of the fact that one dies in one's own world, in the field of own's own meanings. The future as a variety of time is held to be a radical otherness pecisely because "the future of death itself is constituted by its being something totally other [altérité totale]."[37]

In this context another polemical axis gains importance: the relationship to Bergson. We said that Bergson and Sesemann in repeating the latter's thought sought to grasp that reality of time that overcomes its fragmenting into separate moments and varieties. Lévinas also acknowledges that Bergson's conception "preserves the rule of the present over the future: duration is creativity."[38] But Lévinas holds just this to be unacceptable! For it means that in this philosophy death is not reflected upon. But "the futurity [futur] of death determines our future [l'avenir] only insofar as it is not now. It determines what in the future does not fit into any prognosis, any projecting, any impetuous ardor [élan]."[39] Sesemann also marks a difference between futurity and future, but only Lévinas makes this distinction conceptual: futurity isn't the future precisely because the future is a variety of envisaging, whereas futurity is a variety of non-foreseeability. It is just here that otherness lies: futurity cannot be immanentized, subjected to oneself, made one's own.

What are the results of these conclusions that have been reached in a twofold polemical context against the conceptions of both Heidegger and Bergson? "When the present has been robbed of any envisaging, the future loses any kind of common nature [conaturalité]. . . . It is absolutely other and new. It is just in this way that we can grasp the reality of time, the absolute impossibility of finding in the present an analogue of the future, the total nongraspability of the future."[40] Time's reality is here understood not in a Sesemannian way, as a sign of ownness, but as a sign of otherness, not immanently, but transcendentally. This radical conception of the future's otherness is an important guideline for analyzing Sesemann's thought about the other. But before that we should turn our attention to another part of his analysis of time, one that we haven't yet touched on.

The time of the apogee and transcendental otherness

Although Sesemann considers Heidegger's idea about the continuous expansion of ownness into the future and follows Bergson's idea of duration as joining together the moments of existential time, he nevertheless returns to the Augustinian premise that the present moment is special: in the final analysis only the present is actual, existing, and one's own in the true sense of those words. Therefore in seeking the reality of time Sesemann considers the alternative of culture's time and offers another strategy, or perhaps it is an antistrategy. He describes a mindset that differs from the resolute mindset that grounds cultural activity. This is a mindset of alertness. Holding to this mindset, consciousness "does not fling itself about a multitude of temporal moments but keeps being directed to itself at every moment. It is totally mobilized in what is now."[41] A person governed by the attitude of alertness, as opposed to the creator of culture, "does not concern himself with creating an objective culture by subordinating the present moment to the future, but mobilizes his spirit in the present and for the welfare of the present."[42]

In this case the varieties of time group themselves differently than, for example, when one is making an artefact or creating an art work. Keeping to this attitude of consciousness, the person is not oriented toward the future result of his activity or the past resources necessary to reach that goal. Alertness is not a process-related but a momentary thing: "*The past is not a foundation for the present in the way of an already rigidified and crystallized outcome of action but as its subjective dynamism, as a vital source of its inner energy. On the other hand, the future does not stand before the present as a problem that has to be solved, . . . that will replace and transcend it; on the contrary, it is thoroughly marked and determined in the very present, replacing not its dynamics but its statics, that is, the aspect of the present's to-be-competedness and spontaneity.*"[43] The decisive being present of the mindset of alertness is not just one the moments of an activity, as it in the case of an activity oriented toward a stable result; it is self-dependent. Sesemann describes it as "a fullness of vitality and its highest tension."[44]

But in order for the attitude of alertness (as opposed to that of resoluteness) to manifest itself, it by itself is not enough—there has to be an extraordinary circumstance that cannot be created by man's power alone, namely, a limit situation (Grenzsituation). This is a concept introduced by Karl Jaspers, whom Sesemann valued highly. Sesemann talks about special situations of "independent presence," in which "existence suddenly acquires an independent significance and asserts itself at that decisive moment which demands that a human being act *hic et nunc* . . ."[45] In his lecture "Religija ir jos reikšmė pasaulėžiūrai susiformuoti [Religion and its significance for the formation of a worldview]" Sesemann essentially limits all the problematics discussed thus far by describing the level of *ego* as the sphere of immanent experience: "The 'I' is sunk in this [everyday] world in which I live and in which I experience joy and sadness, disappointment and elation, success and failure."[46] But besides that there is another level, that of transcendent experience, which manifests itself in extreme or limit situations.

Such a situation is a thing of unpredictable and ungovernable destiny, and alertness is a mindset necessary for properly facing it. The attitude of alertness and the special givenness of destiny are both conditions for what Sesemann calls the apogee of life, its highest point that brings everything else into focus. The apogee's significant totality is not constituted by distinct temporal moments of biographical time. "The apogee does not at all fit in a row with other moments of existing; it is incommensurate with them and thus depends on neither that life's totality nor on its duration nor on the objective (thing-related) results reached."[47] It is precisely at this exceptional moment that Sesemann's declared goal of *"overcoming imperfect temporality"*[48] and thereby the unreality of existence itself is reached: the apogee is experienced as the most real thing of all. This ecstatic and simultaneously fateful point of time is also a unique point of ownness, in which *I* is *I*. "Only in the apogee is the distractedness and disjointedness of the personality overcome, that incompleteness and unreality, to which it is condemned by the dictatorship of time."[49] On the other hand, the experience of transcendence "tears through and breaks through the closed sphere of immanent experience."[50] The momentary time of the apogee gathers about itself and organizes all other moments of biographical time: focused by it an entire human life takes place, "either waiting for and anticipating it or remembering it as one proceeds on the fated path."[51]

Of course, that second condition for the apogee that I called the fateful given is nothing more than another and peculiar otherness: the challenge of destiny does not depend on the *ego* but essentially constitutes it. Sesemann himself does not treat this topic at length; it can only be reconstructed from other remarks of his. As for Jaspers, the most important of the limit situations for Sesemann was death "as the absolute limit of everyday existence, as the end of immanent experience, as the final destruction of the microcosm whose center is my 'I', as the perishing of our living 'I' connected with the body."[52] It is important to notice that included among the transcendental experiences there is also the already-discussed experience of universal temporality that destroys the reality of existence. In this way we return to the point at which there open up opportunities for alternative attitudes, either of resoluteness or of alertness, and for the overcoming of time's vanishing either through meaningful activity or through a decision in the face of the fateful given.

On a few occasions Sesemann has also written about atemporal transcendence. With respect to existential time this is "something different and otherwordly, where there is no past, no present, and no future, . . . it is the real, unchanging, and perfect reality."[53] Put into this Platonic timeless reality (appealed to without much philosophical preparation), "the temporal being of man turns to nothing. Its center of gravity is placed beyond its limits."[54] In other words, the atemporal otherworldly otherness radically decenters temporal existence. This is a very important thought for our analysis since the acquisition of reality is now no longer connected with ownness, as in all the other arguments of Sesemann that we've discussed, but, on the contrary, it has to do with radical otherness. This is a significant exception, one that pushes Sesemann closest to Lévinas in the latter's thinking about the other and time. At this point we might discern an attempt to push through towards an utterly other.

Unfortunately, Sesemann does not reflect on this theme at greater length, does not analyze the sphere of relevant phenomena; he just mentions that radical otherness quite perfunctorily, for the sake, I might say, of academic correctness. Perhaps this is because of the pedagogical and retrospective nature of his philosophizing: listeners and readers have to be familiarized with what you yourself disagree with and hold to be false, though it has been or still is part of the historical, factual philosophical reality. It is sufficient to recall Kierkegaard's remark about the professor who once in a semester spends an hour in radical Cartesian doubt and then goes on, whereas a genuine doubter's doubt "destroyed reality for him."[55]

Again, it is worthwhile to compare Sesemann's conception of atemporal transcendental otherness with that of Lévinas, which is similar to, and at the same time significantly different from, Sesemann's. Lévinas explicated radical otherness by delving into various thematic fields, by connecting the future with death, mystery, eroticism, and (most significantly for our discussion) with the otherness of another person. In this case transcendence is placed not in an atemporal, perfect reality, but in existential time, which transcendence essentially fractures and turns into something plural and contradictory, so that existence itself must be held to be essentially polychronic. All this is related to a resolute and radical step: the recentering of phenomenological egology. Meanwhile Sesemann, like many other thinkers from Augustine to Kant including some contemporaries (Bergson and Heidegger), does not reflect on the fact that they think about the experience of time in the horizon of the subject, the *I*, that is, the egocentric horizon.

A special situation of confronting the Other, in some respects resembling the one that, according to Sesemann, can determine the apogee of personal time, is described by Lévinas in the axis of an interpersonal relation: when "an event happens to the subject, rather than his taking responsibility for it, he cannot be able to do anything himself, but in a certain way is in the face of that event; this is a relation to another person, [a meeting] face to face with another person, a meeting with a face, giving and at the same time denuding another person."[56] It is in just such a situation that the relation of the present to the future as a radical otherness arises. Essentially this is one and the same relation: "The connection with the future, the future's participation in the present takes place [in the situation] of being face to face with another person. Thus the situation of being face to face is the happening of time itself: the conquest of the future by the present is not an act of a lonely subject (life) but an intersubjective connection. The condition of time is people's relations, or history."[57]

In the context of our deliberations we must observe that Lévinas did not directly tie transcendence, or radical otherness, to its religious or idealist conception, as Sesemann did though, it must be admitted, in a rather superficial and retrospective way. Lévinas did not speak of an eternal, perfect reality, as Sesemann did, thereby preserving elements of Platonism, even though, as we've already seen, he did recognize the totalizing horizon of time to be a guideline for contemporary philosophical thinking. Lévinas, we might say, remained faithful to the requirement to think without abandoning the horizon of time. In that connection he consistently developed an analytic of the relation to the radical Other as an ethical relation to another person, connected otherness with the other person (*l'autrui*), thereby transforming the primarily egocentric phenomenological orientation into a philosophy of the other human being, or the second person. The relation to the other is not a symmetric relation of *I* and *you*, as in the case of Sartre, but a level on which it is impossible to ignore the tie of *I* to oneself and one's ownness. But it is exactly the *you* that becomes for Lévinas the existential first person, so to speak, and thus makes the grammatical first person, the *I*, dependent on the *you*.

This radical overcoming of egocentrism, as we've seen, has an equivalent on the level of time. Sesemann's philosophizing, coming back to timeless transcendence and fundamentally affirming the alliance of religion and idealism, as such thinking has been characterized by Vladimir Lenin, is in this regard very different.

On the purely philosophical plane we must come to the conclusion that the drive towards the Other which I tried to discern and clarify in Sesemann's analyses of time was not consistent: he allows Platonic atemporal reality to intrude into the horizon of time. The emergence of this inclusion is by no means accidental: this can be seen from certain external demands that he made on phenomenological philosophy even though he himself was rather close to it.[58] He thought that phenomenological investigations become truly philosophically significant only if "they are taken in a certain metaphysical perspective, that is, as phenomenological elements of a total [цельное] religiously and ethically justified worldview."[59]

Of course, it might be that Sesemann's purely personal relationship with otherworldliness tacitly provided this retrospective philosophical insert with an appropriate experience. This possibility shall always remain what is banally referred to as another soul's secret. In his archive there is a prayer, written in a childish hand in Swedish, but it does not unravel this mystery. The clothes of retrospective philosophical thinking cover but do not abolish it. The religious-idealist compound hides both of its components in such a way that it becomes difficult if not utterly impossible to determine which of them is really active in one or another case. But the secret remains, and that is no longer an object of philosophical deliberation and not an argument for or against.

Endnotes

1   More extensive biographical information can be found in Thorsten Botz-Bornstein, *Vasily Sesemann. Experience, formalism, and the question of being*, Amsterdam, New York: Rodopi, 2006, p. 119–121; Arūnas Sverdiolas, "Une tentative pour se frayer un chemin vers l'autre: Vassili Sezeman," in Françoise Lesourd (ed.), *L'altérité. Etudes sur la pensée russe*, Lyon: Université Jean Moulin Lyon 3, 2007, p. 175–176.
2   Thorsten Botz-Bornstein, *Vasily Sesemann. Experience, formalism, and the question of being*, Amsterdam, New York: Rodopi, 2006.
3   Cf. Vasily Sesemann, *Aesthetics*, Amsterdam, New York: Rodopi, 2007.
4   Cf. Николай Лосский, *История русской философии*, Москва: Советский писатель, 1991, p. 375–376. (1st edition, 1951). It seems that Lossky was acquainted with by no means all of Sesemann's works.
5   Василий Сеземан, "M. Heidegger.—Sein und Zeit. I. 1927," *Путь*, 1928, nr. 14, p. 117.
6   Cf. Thorsten Botz-Bornstein, *Vasily Sesemann. Experience, formalism, and the question of being*, p. 21.
7   This is how Sesemann is presented by Thomas Nemeth in his article "Russian Neo-Kantians," in *Routledge Encyclopedia of Philosophy*, Cambridge and New York, 1998, vol. 8.
8   Emmanuel Lévinas, *De l'existence a l'existant*, Paris: J. Vrin, 1978, p. 160.
9   Emmanuel Lévinas, *Le temps et l'autre*, Paris: PUF, 1983, p. 64.
10 Ibid., p. 17.
11 See Vosylius Sezemanas, *Logika*, Kaunas: Humanitarinių mokslų fakulteto leidinys, 1929, p. 144–148.
12 See Vosylius Sezemanas, *Pažinimo problema*, in *Raštai. Gnoseologija*, Vilnius: Mintis, 1987, p. 189–190.
13 Ibid., p. 190.
14 Vosylius Sezemanas, "Mūsų laikų gnoseologijai naujai orientuojantis" in *Raštai. Gnoseologija*, Vilnius: Mintis, 1987, p. 344.
15 Vosylius Sezemanas, "Das Problem des Idealismus in der Philosophie" in *Lietuvos universiteto humanitarinių mokslų fakulteto raštai*, Bk.1, Kaunas, 1925.

16 A somewhat earlier Russian version was published as [В. Чухнин], "Время, культура и тело: К познанию культурных задач современности," Тридцатые годы: Утверждение евразийцев. Париж. 1931, с. 147–189; I was unsuccessful in finding it.
17 Vosylius Sezemanas, "Laikas, kultūra ir kūnas" in *Raštai. Filosofijos istorija. Kultūra*, Vilnius: Mintis, 1997, p. 568.
18 Ibid., p. 569.
19 Ibid.
20 Vosylius Sezemanas, "Heidegger Martinas," in *Raštai. Filosofijos istorija. Kultūra*, Vilnius: Mintis, 1997, p. 323–324.
21 Василий Сеземан, "M. Heidegger.—Sein und Zeit." I. 1927, p. 120–121.
22 Vosylius Sezemanas, "Heidegger Martinas," p. 322, 324.
23 Vosylius Sezemanas, "Laikas, kultūra ir kūnas," p. 569.
24 Ibid., p. 572–573.
25 Vosylius Sezemanas, "Laikas, kultūra ir kūnas," p. 573.
26 Василий Сеземан, "M. Heidegger.—Sein und Zeit. I. 1927," p. 121.
27 Ibid.
28 See Arūnas Sverdiolas, *Kultūros filosofija Lietuvoje*, Vilnius: Mintis, 1983.
29 Vosylius Sezemanas, "Laikas, kultūra ir kūnas," p. 575.
30 Ibid., p. 578.
31 Ibid., p. 582–583.
32 Ibid., p. 583.
33 Ibid.
34 Ibid., p. 588.
35 Василий Сеземан, "M. Heidegger.—Sein und Zeit." I. 1927, p. 121.
36 Emmanuel Lévinas, *Le temps et l'autre*, Paris: PUF, 1983, p. 64
37 Ibid., p. 74.
38 Ibid., p. 72.
39 Ibid., p. 71.
40 Ibid.
41 Vosylius Sezemanas, "Laikas, kultūra ir kūnas," p. 593.
42 Ibid., p. 596–597.
43 Ibid., p. 597.
44 Ibid.
45 Ibid., p. 583.
46 Vosylius Sezemanas, "Religija ir jos reikšmė pasaulėžiūrai susiformuoti," in *Raštai. Filosofijos istorija. Kultūra*, Vilnius: Mintis, 1997, p. 663.
47 Vosylius Sezemanas, "Laikas, kultūra ir kūnas," p. 598.
48 Ibid., p. 599.
49 Ibid., p. 601.
50 Vosylius Sezemanas, "Religija ir jos reikšmė pasaulėžiūrai susiformuoti," p. 664.
51 Vosylius Sezemanas, "Laikas, kultūra ir kūnas," p. 598.
52 Vosylius Sezemanas, "Religija ir jos reikšmė pasaulėžiūrai susiformuoti," p. 664.
53 Vosylius Sezemanas, "Laikas, kultūra ir kūnas," p. 570.

54 Ibid., p. 570.
55 Søren Kierkegaard, *Baimė ir drebėjimas*, vertė Jolita Adomėnienė, Vilnius: Aidai, 2002, p. 103.
56 Emmanuel Lévinas, *Le temps et l'autre*, p. 67.
57 Ten pat, p. 68–69.
58 Cf. Vosylius Sezemanas, "Fenomenas," "Fenomenologija," "Heidegger Martinas," "Husserl Edmundas" in *Raštai. Filosofijos istorija. Kultūra* (ed. Loreta Anilionytė), Vilnius: Mintis, 1997.
59 Василий Сеземан, "M. Heidegger.—Sein und Zeit. I. 1927," p. 123.

AESTHETIC EVALUATION IN THE HISTORY OF ART
(On the Relation between Art History and Aesthetics)

I

One of the most characteristic features of contemporary scholarship is its methodological orientation, as if the Cartesian spirit of doubt and self-doubt had been reborn in it. The scientific thought of today does not confine its attention exclusively to the thing that has entered its purview. Rather, it ceaselessly reviews and tests the whole arsenal of available methods and modes of thought, striving to make them ever more graceful and perfect, sometimes even changing them fundamentally.

But there are also essential differences between the methodological orientation of Cartesian philosophy and that of our times. For 17th century rationalism the most urgent concern was the unity of scientific knowledge (method). Through the authenticity and objective significance of reason and its laws it endeavored to ground the universality of scientific method. Contemporary thought, on the other hand, without neglecting the common elements of scientific knowledge, is more concerned with a precise delimitation of the separate fields of knowledge and their proper objects. This explains the two-fold direction of contemporary scientific methodology. On the one hand, its researches plumb the most basic logical foundations of knowledge; on the other, it emphasizes an especially attentive and intimate relationship to the factual level of the science, i.e., to the peculiar way each objective datum it analyzes has being. And even though at first sight both of these problems relate to different aspects of the science, every concrete effort to solve them discloses their inner connection.

The same holds for the history of art and literature. The methodological tendency of contemporary thought has fruitfully benefited it too. Only now does this science, after a long and barren period of disorientation, begin to discover itself and to comprehend its true vocation and object. But in distinguishing itself and its object from nearby and akin disciplines, the history of art (and of literature) has to answer two questions, (1) What is its place in the system of sciences, i.e., in what other discipline is its grounding to be found? and (2) What are the characteristics and peculiarities of its object? It is not difficult upon deeper investigation to conclude that both these questions are organically related.

II

Indeed, what is the history of art (understood in a wide sense to include that of fiction and poetry as well)?

First, it is a science of *history* and therefore has to satisfy all the methodological requirements of any historical discipline. This means that the history of art, like that of anything else, investigates not individual works of art but the way this or that art form changes organically over time in the context of its being and evolution; and it also attempts to detect in this process a certain inner unity and regularity peculiar to it. Only so can it perform its main task, which is to explain the present by the past, i.e., to connect them causally and to discern in the present the seeds and potentialities of the future. Nevertheless, art history must not limit its purview to studying only the evolution of art itself. It should not leave out of account the unity and continuity of cultural life (with all its phenomena) as a whole. Thus, in order correctly to understand the historical destiny of art itself, it is necessary to determine how it is related to all other areas of cultural life.

Today these considerations sound like truisms. They have entered the lifeblood of contemporary history of art, and everything that has been accomplished in it during the last few decades has consisted almost without exception of investigations into the connections between art history and developments in other areas of cultural life.

Yet this concerns only one side of the issue. The other, equally important issue has been effectively forgotten or, at the very least, its methodological significance has largely been ignored. Namely, all sciences, including that of history, have to accord, both in their methods and in their foundations, with the special nature of the problems being analyzed. Otherwise they will not contain information about reality, i.e., information about facts.

Applying this to the history of art, we get the result that it is crucial for its methodical structure that it is *art* in particular of which it is the history. Thus it must, of necessity, concern itself with the special qualities of art itself; it must seek its support and ground in the general theory of art, in the philosophy of art or aesthetics. But this grounding of art history in aesthetics usually elicits the most strenuous objections, above all from art specialists themselves. Aesthetics is held to be a normative discipline that provides artistic taste with general rules of aesthetic valuation. To found art history on aesthetics would entail requiring that the object to be analyzed be judged, and this is considered to be incompatible with the art history's scientific dignity. Any judgment or valuation, especially an aesthetic one, is relative, subjective, and determined by historically changing circumstances;

therefore it lacks any objective universal significance. Hence the history of art, if it wants to be a science in the strict sense of the word, must follow the example of the natural sciences and avoid all value judgments.

Such a view, one that assimilates artistic along with all other cultural phenomena to simple facts, to natural phenomena, was most forthrightly and consistently expounded in the theory of *Hippolyte Taine*. He tried to explain historical types of artistic creation as facts of culture by their social environment: the individual features of their creators' race, the climate, and so on. Even putting aside Taine, the judgment-eschewing naturalist position still retains its importance for art history. Basically it is not at all opposed to the newly emergent tasks of art history. Focusing on art forms, it only explains their changes and continuities; the dependence of some of them on others; and the differences in the nature and combination of factors that give rise to these forms. Raphael or Pushkin are studied only as the creators of certain artistic styles just as Giulio Romano or Nikolai Nekrasov are, regardless of whether they were major, independent artistic figures or insignificant epigones.

We will not proceed to criticize Taine's theory at length here.[1] The fundamental deficiency of this theory is not that its explanations of the development and change of artistic styles are unfounded, but that in speaking about art Taine circumvents the art phenomena and their peculiarities themselves. This appears to be no accident but the natural consequence of the equal sign that Taine places between the phenomenon of art and the physical phenomenon. Thus the methodological foundation of art history cannot avoid the question, How justified is such an identification of art and natural science? In truth, does there exist an art form that gives some creation an artistic nature in the same sense that a physical or chemical property gives something a physical or chemical nature? The reality of the latter becomes a fact for us insofar as we sensibly perceive them, i.e., see, hear, smell, etc. them. Yet this is by no means sufficient for the perception of an art form. To hear a musical piece, to see a painting, to read a poem is not yet to grasp it as a phenomenon of art. One can hold a Madonna by Raphael or a portrait by Rembrandt to be a picture of the Mother of God or of a man without any connection to art, just as an unmusical person can hear music without taking it to be, and understanding it as, a work of musical art.

Hence it is evident that the sensory object which we call a work of art (a painted canvas, a printed poem, a musical score) is not yet a finished aesthetic object, since the perceiver can endow it with different meanings (artistic and non-artistic). The external given is only the sensory basis and material from which the real aesthetic object is created. In other words, this object is realized only by what Boder Christiansen has aptly called a secondary creative act, i.e., a living artistic apprehension. Consequently we can righfully speak of a special aesthetic reality that does not coincide with the empirical reality of everyday experience. On the empirical level a piece of music is equally real to both a musical and a non-musical listener. But only the perception enjoyed by the former actualizes its aesthetic reality.

Usually the nature of the aesthetic object is characterized somewhat differently. It is said that its structure is determined by two distinct factors, one of them being objective and consisting of the picture's, statue's, building's, etc. sensory given, the other being subjective as indicated by my relation to it, my conscious attitude toward it, which gives it a certain color and thanks to which that given acquires a unique value and a certain emotional content. But this characterization distorts somewhat the real essence of the matter.

First, the distinction between the subjective and the objective factor results not from an initial reflection on these things, but from theory. Moreover, it is phenomenologically unjustified, since in an immediate artistic perceptions both these moments constitute an indivisible, objective totality. This peculiar objective totality just is the aesthetic reality, all of which does not fit into the framework of the conventional view that divides reality into subjective and objective.

And what conclusions follow from our phenomenological point of view? If it is correct, i.e., if the aesthetic object is a sovereign reality manifesting itself in a living aesthetic perception, then it follows it can be known and understood only in a direct creative act of perception caused by the object as it is experienced. And this act inevitably contains an *evaluative* moment. In truth, we conceive artistic form in no other way than by recognizing it as an aesthetic value, i.e., by evaluating it aesthetically. Without such a valuational act the artistic form would not be real as an aesthetic phenomenon at all. True, this is an evaluation of an exceptional kind: it is unconditional and hence categorical; it only identifies and recognizes an aesthetic value, placing aesthetic being against nonaesthetic being, without undertaking any internal grading within the aesthetic sphere itself. Thus, for instance, the perception of a Beethoven sonata or a Velazquez painting is only a recognition and confirmation of their being aesthetically valuable without any determination of their aesthetic ranking.

III

Finally we can approach the question we raised earlier. Can the history of *art* avoid any kind of evaluation? Obviously, it cannot. It's already clear that inevitably it envisages the uncondidional, categorical evaluation we've mentioned; otherwise it would lose its object, artistic form, which, as we've seen, becomes an objective reality only thanks to this act of recognizing and confirming its aesthetic value.

But that is not all. The history of art not only envisages an unconditional evaluation as an inevitable transcendent fact prior to its own purview but inevitably incorporates it within itself as the only legitimate starting point for all its investigations. It is only in this way that art history fulfills the requirements placed on any science that analyzes real facts: to base itself on the *primary data* that constitute the foundation of those facts. And these primary data with respect to artistic form are provided by the actual artistic perception, i.e., the experience based on the unconditional act of aesthetic evaluation.

By contrast, the knowledge about the mere possibility or even fact of a simple evaluation, which knowledge neither re-creates nor actualizes that evaluation, is already secondary and derivative. Or, to use Christiansen's terminology, every heteronomous evaluation presupposes an autonomous evaluation.

At first sight, this claim might seem paradoxical: doesn't art history proceed exactly contrariwise? Doesn't it eschew any kind of autonomous evaluation and limit itself to a heteronomous one, investigating only those paintings, sculptures, poems, musical and other compositions whose artistic value is either universally recognized or has been recognized by those epchochs and cultures in which they were created? But in reality this independence of art history from the actual (autonomous) evaluation is purely illusory. Let's say the primary fact is held to be the externally real thing or creation before the art historian's eyes (a printed poem, a painted canvas, an architectural building). Now, as we've seen, this outward creation is just some stuff that, before it can acquire aesthetic significance, must first be properly explicated, endowed with meaning; i.e., it presupposes a live aesthetic perception tied to an unconditional valuation. And if we say that the fact of aesthetic perception and explication is something guven to us in finished form, i.e., if we base ourselves on our knowledge about the acts of meaning-endowment and explication performed by other authorities or epochs, then we will clearly transgress against the spirit of pure and critical scholarship. That would be exchanging the primary fact for a secondary and derivative one; it would be taking the primary source and substituting second-hand or third-hand news for it. The inadequacy of this is especially evident in those cases where art history (as inevitably happens) comes upon forgotten or unrecognized art works.

In such cases there is no heteronomous valuation, or its verdict is negative. But only an unconditional, autonomous evaluation, i.e., one proceeding from a pure aesthetic perception, is capable of revealing (recovering) the real and positive aesthetic value of these art works that the judgment of history has slighted. Yet even leaving aside these comparatively rare exceptional cases, heteronomous valuation cannot be a starting datum for history. For every alien explication and interpretation of any facts whatsoever requires our own appropriate understanding and explication of them. Therefore, heteronomous evaluation, if it is to be justified, must seek to re-create that autonomous valuation from which it once (i.e., at a certain epoch and in a certain group of people) arose.

All these considerations seem to show sufficiently clearly that an art historian's work must be based on an immediate aesthetic perception in the unconditional sense indicated. Thus abstractly formulated this claim will hardly meet with any opposition from historians of art and literature, though in concrete cases of artistic analysis its import is rarely fully appreciated or even noticed. Otherwise there wouldn't occur so many cases in which instead of an artistic analysis of a work of visual art or poetry (especially if it hails from antiquity) we get descriptions of an archaeological or cultural-historical nature; or cases in which textual criticism correcting distortions found in the manuscript tradition and providing this or that interpolation is guided first and foremost by logically rational rather than aesthetic criteria. In these cases it is evidently forgotten that aesthetic analysis has to be directly consequent upon aesthetic perception and to be based upon the data revealed in it; i.e., that aesthetic perception and aesthetic valuation are immanent to aesthetic analysis rather than being transcendent with respect to it.

Only insofar as it adheres to this condition will the history of art be enabled to fulfill one of its main tasks: to provide the key of today to a genuine understanding of art works of the past; to indicate the right attitude toward them and to ascertain the mental set necessary for such an attitude; in other words, to do something analogous to what a performer and especially a conductor does when by the magic of his revelatory interpretations he opens our ears to a distinct appreciation of those musical works whose unique value and meaning has hitherto escaped us. For Beethoven's Ninth it was Hans von Bülow who provided such a revelation, and for the works of Tchaikovsky and Bruckner it was Arthur Nikisch. Only that interpreter or art historian can explain a work of art who feels empathy with it, i.e., who in his explanation bases himself on an immediate artistic perception founded on an unconditional valuation.

The essential importance of grounding aesthetic analysis on an immediate artistic perception, which was never questioned in the history and theory of music, has now started being grasped by historians of other fields of artistic creativity. For example, contemporary literary history focuses on the melodicity of this or that poet's verses. Obviously the artistic significance of the factors that determine melodicity (e.g., vocal intonation and dynamics, speed and manner of reading) can be gauged only in case the starting point of the analysis is a declamation of the poem and the artistic impression it creates.

If the poem is analyzed only as a printed thing for one's eyes, its melodic moment doesn't exist and remains unrealized. One more example: the analysis of architectural style requires that works exemplifying it be perceived under a certain lighting from a certain distance, and so on.

There are cases when a real understanding of the art of bygone eras is granted to us by present-day art. Thus the newest French art of painting has taught us to perceive and appreciate the artistry of the old Russian icons. Obviously, the latter again became alive and comprehensible for us because we started to base ourselves on an *immediate* present *perception* of it.

IV

But this does not yet exhaust the role of aesthertic evaluation in art history. It is possible to acknowledge that any aesthetic analysis of a work of art confronts the unconditional evaluation, which is absolutely necessary, and at the same time to deny to art history the right to a standard evaluation, which is a relative, comparative judgment that does not delimit artistic objects from non-artistic ones but only determines, within the limits of aestheticity, a greater or lesser degree of artistic quality. If it cannot be disputed that a historical-literary analysis of Pushkin is inevitably based on an artistic perception and comprehension of his works, it does not at all follow that the history of literature, as an exact science, must take up the question, Who is the greater poet, Pushkin or Lermontov? The latter is a problem for literary criticism, which is guided by whatever criteria you like other than objective scientific ones.

But this question is not so simple as might appear at first glance because the concept of evaluation itself harbors a certain unclarity and ambiguity. Therefore, so as to avoid any misunderstandings, it is necessary to clarify in general to what extent and in what sense a scientifically grounded analysis of art works is possible. For it seems that the concept of such an analysis contains an insoluble contradiction, that within it there clash two requirements that negate each other.

On the one hand, art by its very nature is incompatible with scientific analysis. Each work of art is a self-sufficient unit; it is a closed little world whose value does not depend on the surrounding universe. Whoever wants to enter it and understand it, must devote himself to it completely, immersing himself in it and forgetting everything outside it. Such features of works of art and their perception in aesthetic contemplation were called attention to by Kant and Schopenhauer; and in our times they were emphasized by the so-called theory of aesthetic isolation that characterized the difference between scientific cognition and artistic contemplation as follows: the latter does not include its object into the system of the universe but, on the contrary, separates and isolates it. And it is just this distinctive feature of works of art—their organic value and closure—that is irreconcilable with scientific analysis and comparison. Analysis demolishes the work of art, chops it up into parts and thereby destroys its vitality as a whole, its internal unity; while comparison inevitably depends on illustration by similitude, determination of affinities, all of which negate the closure and separateness peculiar to a work of art.

On the other hand, the history of art, as a type of scientific knowledge, is by its essence dependent on reflection and the analysis based on it. When it investigates works of art, it doesn't take them separately and abstractly, but puts them in rows of teleological order and then analyzes them in terms of the development and change of their artistic styles in certain epochs. Here analysis and comparison condition and support one another. The purpose of analysis is comparison; and comparison in turn provides new starting points for analysis.

How does art history manage to unite and reconcile within itself these two contradictory requirements, one of which arises from its object and the other from its method? Even if it's is true that the scientific method must adjust itself to the nature of the object being investigated, it doesn't follow that it must renounce its nature as a cognitive activity that compares and analyzes. So how does one move in art history from artistic contemplation to scholarly reflection, from one mindset to another, if it is imperative to preserve both the peculiarities of the object and the sctrictness of the scientific method? Perhaps the best answer can be given by appeal to a simple analogy. The just-mentioned move may be compared to translating from one language (that of artistic impressions) to another (that of scholarly concepts). What conditions must be met if the translation is to convey the original faithfully? We may mention two. First, it is necessary for the translator to know both languages equally well; for him to have an equally accurate and subtle understanding of, and feel for, the one and the other language. In the case at hand this means that the art historian must at the same time be both a subtle judge of art (i.e., be capable of genuine aesthetic perception) and a scholarly thinker. This condition is evident and requires no further explanation.

Things are not so straightforward with the second condition, which requires that there be a certain correspondence between the structures of both languages; i.e., that all structural elements of the one be adequately expressible in those of the other. Is there such a correspondence between the language of artistic impressions and the language of scientific concepts? This is the question on answering which the possibility of scientifically analyzing works of art depends.

If the aesthetic object were truly wholly indivisible, unitary, and internally homogeneous, as is sometimes asserted, then the analysis of its aesthetic side would in principle be impossible, for it would in any case destroy that toward which it is directed; it would decompose the aesthetic object into parts, elements, or factors, of which none would have any aesthetic value. This value would inhere only in the object as a whole and just in it alone regardless of its relation to anything else. But in truth this is not so. Every aesthetic object is not only a finished whole; it is also characterized by a certain internal complexity (a unity-preserving variety of distinct elements)—and this in a twofold sense.

First of all, the aesthetic object is a totality, decomposable into more or less self-sufficient parts which, though dependent on that totality, do not lose their own special aesthetic significance. One can see this particularly well in such art forms as music and poetry, where the whole does not disclose itself at once but is created gradually in the process of perception. If this process were absolutely homogeneous and continuous during all of its moments, the aesthetic effect would be realized only at the end of the process. But actually in both music and poetry the very process of creating (perceiving) the object is aesthetically significant. And this is possible only because the totality emerges gradually from the constituent and alternating parts, each of which, aesthetically speaking, is *conditionally* complete and homogeneous. This inner decomposition and organization of musical and poetical works is the reason why the past stays in the present and at the same time provides a certain impulse to the perception of the future.

On the other hand, the internal structure of the aesthetic object is thereby not yet sufficiently described. This object is not only a whole consisting of parts but also a certain type of compositional unity arising from a multitude of interweaving and interfusing factors and moments (partly independent, partly rooted one in the other) that interact amongst themselves. For example, in poetry it is a phonetic, rhythmic, syntactic, and semantic structure; in music we have a melodic picture, polyphony, harmonization, rhythm, instrumentation, and emotional content; in painting there are the drawing, color, composition (the arrangement of masses on the canvas surface), the meaning-related and emotional moment, and so on. Each of these factors is aesthetically real and significant only in relation to other factors as a moment of compositional unity. Yet these separate factors do not dissolve in the whole, which only provides the background for their acquiring a peculiar aesthetic meaning that is brought to consciousness in a vital artistic perception. This inner structural multifacetedness of the aesthetic object means that from an artistic point of view not all of its factors have the same comparative weight. Its immediately perceived unity, as a phenomenological analysis shows, is achieved by the fact that one of the factors gets a leading role; the aesthetic stress falls on it; and it becomes, as Christiansen aptly observes, a *dominant* to which all the other factors submit and to whose aesthetic significance they adjust.

The difficulties one sometimes faces in aesthetically grasping works of art arise precisely from the fact one doesn't always arrive at a correct view of an aesthetic object, doesn't always find the "dominant" that determines the object's internal structure. This property of the aesthetic object, its compositional multifacetedness and organization, just is the necessary foundation for art history when works of art ar analyzed. In a correct analysis the artistic creation is by no means divided into parts and elements that are foreign to it and aesthetically meaningless (as is done, for example, in a philological or archaeological analysis); rather, what are revealed and captured in scientific terminology are just those elements or moments that subsist in the very essence of the aesthetic object. In other words, scientific analysis directly (immanently) arises from artistic perception and is an objective interpretation of its aesthetic significance.

V

If it is taken as established that a scientific analysis of the aesthetic object is possible and if the general methods of that analysis have been described, then the conditions are set for answering the principal question of this investigation: Is this analysis conditioned by an aesthetic judgment? And if so, then in what sense?

The most important conclusion of our explorations hitherto has been that art history is premised on an unconditioned (categorical) aesthetic evaluation, for art history is—or at least ought to be—based on an immediate artistic perception. Now that conclusion may be made more precise: artistic perception conditions not only the in-principle possibility of a scientific analysis of works of art but also all possible directions this analysis can take, for only artistic perception can determine which aesthetic factors or moments are to be analyzed and only aesthetic perception can guarantee the completeness and legitimacy of such an analysis.

If, in keeping with the traditional attitude, we begin our analysis not with a live artistic perception but with the external givenness of a work of art (the printed poem, the printed score, the colors and lines on the surface of the canvas, etc.), as art historians usually do when they mistake heteronomous evaluation for the absence of any evaluation at all, then, it is true, *some* aesthetic factors in this external object can be immediately perceived and acknowledged (e. g., rhymes in poetry, rhythm and harmony in music, color and composition in painting, etc.), but *only* some; because others, no less important, will remain unobserved precisely because they are actualized only in the correlation formed between the perceiving subject and external object in an immediate artistic perception (e. g., the nature of the dominant in one or another complex of elements).

Thus we see that it is only the unconditioned valuation inherent in an artistic perception that indicates the guidelines which art history must go by in analyzing works of art. Any investigation that is not guided by this valuation *ipso facto* does not belong to art history, strictly conceived. It is merely auxiliary and without independent significance; its goal is just to gather and to prepare an aesthetically uninformed raw material for the compositional analysis that is the principal task of art history. Such auxiliary disciplines include all those various investigations the objects of which are, for example, the history of the technical means used by the arts, biographical data about an artist's life and work, accounts of the general cultural influences upon him, and so on.

But if it is the usual view of art historians that both these disciplines as well as the analysis of artistic form, the kernel of art history, have nothing to do with evaluation, then this view is, as we have seen, an illusion, but one that rests on a real foundation.

There is first of all the covert and unconscious feature of unconditional evaluation whereby it seems to the investigator that in analyzing a work of art he is basing himself only on the externally available sensory data, whereas in fact he is unwittingly supplementing his analysis with features and moments that are not sensorily given but still part of an immediate artistic perception.

In addition, the very nature of unconditional evaluation (its categoricalness) makes it hard to be taken as such. An investigator is called upon to judge both good and bad works of art, and both require a special aesthetical mindset. The only difference is that in one case this requirement is satisfied, whereas in the other it just remains as a requirement, meaning either that the artistic perrception does not take place at all or it is not integral and unified. Hence the often expressed opinion that the scientific analysis of works of art must orient itself to perfect examples of the art is quite natural. This is important not because for the sake of popularity this analysis must be based on general agreement (*consensus omnium*) but because only perfect examples are able to actualize an integral artistic perception to its fullest extent.

Finally we may mention one more factor peculiar to all investigations of art history, due to which factor the impression arises that judgment is alien to them. When the unconditional evaluation (tacit or conscious) has already taken place and the investigation has been steered in the proper direction, the formal analysis of the work of art itself (at least initially) is not evaluative in nature, for its primary task is to provide a *general* description of the artistic forms and methods characteristic of the art being investigated. Such a morphology of art indeed limits itself to a simple listing of all the structural elements of an artistic composition, with no evaluation og them.

However, a general morphology of art works is not yet a stylistic analysis of them in the true sense of the word, i.e., an analysis of artistic form. So if formal investigations of art history confine themselves to morphology, they deserve the accusation that is frequently leveled at them, viz., that they fail to grap what is most important in a work of art, its "spirit." For a simple listing of artistic methods and compositional devices does not yet reveal and justify their artistic meaning or aesthetic significance. Indeed, a full description of the artistic form is not given by noting the presence of certain devices underlying that form. For other products of cultural creativity (e.g., technological objects, practical or scientific language) also make use of similar or even the same devices. Thus, meter and rhyme are used both in works of poetry and in rules of language (especially Latin). But in one case they are an artistic and in the other a memonic device.

That is not all. Even within the realm of art one and the same element can have a distinct meaning; thus, Slavicisms in Russian poetry before Pushkin meant a different thing from what they mean in Pushkin's work; columns in Renaissance architecture have a different meaning than in Baroque structures. Furthermore, neither an artistic element taken separately nor a certain complex of them is insufficient by itself to make a work of art valuable. An artist can use the same elements either masterfully or incompetently, i.e., create both good and poor works of art by their means.

What then grounds the aesthetic significance of an art work's factors or elements if it is not to be found in them taken separately? The answer to this question emerges from the above-mentioned structural and organic unity that works of art possess. Elements and factors exist only in the art work taken as a whole; therefore, their significance arises out of their relation to the compositional whole. This relation is a relation of means to end; but those means do not enter the whole only to dissolve in it; they have not only an auxiliary but also an independent significance. This *teleological* structure of the aesthetic object is particularly clearly discernible if analyzed from the viewpoint of the creative process. Separate factors or elements emerge here as special creative ways of embodying a certain artistic idea. Now the meaning of each such way of creating can only be conceived and determined *teleologically*, that is, with regard to its greater or lesser suitability to the artistic task at hand. In other words, to understand the aesthetic significance of the separate artistic factors or ways one needs a certain teleologically based evaluation, which is equivalent to a simple (categorical) recognition of their value, i.e., one that isn't closed and unconditional.

Thus in the greater or lesser appropriateness of the factors or ways to the total artistic idea there already lies a comparative, gradational moment, which permits the possibility of judging the relative perfection of the aesthetic object's teleological structure. This judgment is first of all made by the creative artist himself. It is a long and sometimes arduous task to settle upon the final form of an art work; this involves a continuous process of making the work ever more perfect, of discarding whatever fails to satisfy the conditions of the work's fundamental artistic idea; and these creative labor pains are marked by the sign of teleological (comparative) judgment. For example, the replacement of one synonym with another in a poem or the choice of one harmonic transition over another in a musical piece is determined and justified only by a higher degree of its teleological perfection, i.e., something that conditions its aesthetic superiority in that particular case. Hence, this evaluation is inevitably made not only by the creative artist himself but also more or less consciously and explicitly by anyone who aesthetically perceives his creation. Therefore, if in his investigations the art historian always must base himself on an immediate artistic perception, then the elucidation of this *comparative* evaluation (together with the determination of its objective foundations) is also part of his reflexive analysis.

The comparative nature of the aesthetic judgment in question shows up even more clearly and perspicuously when art history moves from analysing individual works of art to grouping them together based on their teleological structure (i.e., their relative aesthetic perfection). The commonality of inner structure (in terms of artistic composition and principal factors) of art works of the same kind leads quite naturally and invariably to such a comparative aesthetic evaluation.

This comparative evaluation is an important stage in the methodical development of the history and evolution of art; and it is only because of it that the specifically historical nature of this discipline becomes evident. For as long as the latter is restricted to the morphology of art forms, the investigations remain within the sphere of general schemes and artificial abstractions. But only when art history begins to analyze specific works of art do these schemes acquire content and become real historical phenomena. It is only these concrete embodiments that enable the researcher to reveal the true aesthetic aspect of the works of art, i.e., their artistic style; for, as we've already seen, the aesthetic significance of the various factors and moments of artistic form actualizes itself only when these are conjoined with other factors and moments into a certain compositional whole, all in the course of in one way or another executing a certain artistic task.

Methodically this transition from morphology to stylistics (stylistic analysis) manifests itself in the fact that the investigations of the art historian cease to be exclusively analytic: analysis is supplemented by synthesis, the task of which is to reveal the supreme unity that ties all aesthetic factors into one compositional whole that becomes evident in an immediate aesthetic perception.

This synthesis is strictly teleological; it is accompanied by that comparative aesthetic valuation (judgment) that we discussed earlier.

VI

But even all this does not yet fully define the task and object of art history. Its center of gravity, as the comparative valuation shows, is not the elucidation of *individual* art works, but the disclosure of an internal connection between whole classes and groups of them. In truth, art history analyzes each art work not in abstraction from the others but as a phenomenon characteristic of a certain epoch's aesthetic spirit which determines its peculiar artistic style. This spirit or, more precisely, this aesthetic mindset is not just a simple totality of all the art works of that period, but a living potentiality (not only as mere possibility but also as effective power and force) giving birth to all of a particular epoch's artistic creations and expressing in them all the vicissitudes of its own development, its own rise and fall. This is the true object of the history of art, an object essentially woven out of valuational and teleological moments. Being a certain tendency of the aesthetic consciousness, this potentiality expresses—via a valuation (judgment)—its relation to less valuable works of art; and in order that it itself be understood it demands a similar valuational (judgmental) relation with respect to itself[2]. Of course, in the order of scholarly research it is something secondary and derivative, for it is art history that creates it on the basis of the data at its disposal, i.e., various works of art and the comparison thereof. Even so it is an independent object having its own reality whose objective unity can be perceived only by immediately grasping and immersing oneself into the aesthetic style of the epoch in question. Its peculiarity resides in its ability to evoke a special attitude of aesthetic consciousness different from the attitude required by a single work of art grasped as a closed totality. And this difference is gounded precisely on acts of comparing art works of the same style, acts that are performed by the art historian in his reflections. It makes a huge difference whether we analyze Goethe's *Faust* or Pushkin's *Eugene Onegin* as freestanding works of literature or as products of a certain epoch and its aesthetic strivings. Of course, even an ordinary undertanding of *Faust* or *Eugene Onegin* requires some knowledge of the epoch and its style. But in that case this knowledge performs only an auxiliary role; it is so to speak a neutral background which helps to actualize fully the aesthetic experience of the work.

In doing history of art the aesthetic perspective changes radically. Here this background enters into the foreground as a living creative potentiality, whereas the individual art works are analyzed solely in relation to this foreground; i.e., as its more or less perfect and typical manifestations[3]. The difference between these two aesthetic mindsets sometimes very clearly manifests itself as an incongruity between the aesthetic judgments relevant to each. This is shown by the following example.

One of the most important moments of significance determining aesthetic contemplation is the creative freedom that reveals itself in a work of art. This freedom, as was correctly noted by Kant and Schelling, harmonizes in a special way with the inner lawlikeness and necessity of artistic composition. Where there is no such incomparably unique coincidence of freedom and necessity, there just is no art. Where there is no necessity, there can be no self-complete compositional unity. Where there is no freedom, there the place of creativity is taken over by pure mechanics. In this way all creations both utterly chaotic and arbitrary as well as those absolutely, univocally mechanical remain beyond the purview of real art.[4] An immediate perception of this creative freedom in artistic contemplation depends, as Christiansen has shown, on so-called differential sensations, i.e., on perceiving not only the art works' peculiarity, the uniqueness of the ways and means whereby the artist achieves their compositional unity, but also their power (contrast-determined vividness) or inner tension and concentration. These differential sensations do not always create the aesthetic object to the same degree or extent. When the aesthetic attitude is oriented toward a specific work of art as a self-enclosed totality, the role of differential sensations is more modest and limited compared to the case when aesthetic contemplation is directed toward the artistic potentiality of an entire epoch, a potentiality discernible only upon comparing various works in a group of the same kind. In the latter case the repeated appearance of one and the same artistic means in all works of this group can call forth a negative differential sensation, i.e., an impression that this artistic means is being applied only mechanically; whereas these same works analyzed without comparing one to the other appear truly artistic, born of a free creativity. Thus the difference in artistic evaluation here is conditioned by the just-mentioned difference in the aesthetic mindset (the attitude of the aesthetic consciousness). This helps explain the negative view that the the Baroque period had of the strict rhythmicity and symmetry characteristic of Renaissance architectural forms or the *enjambement* that the French romanticists carried into the Alexandrine couplet in place of the strict coincidence of syntactical and rhythmic units prevalent in the work of their Classicist predecessors. In essence this also explains the difference between the way late Greek sculptures and their Roman imitations (copies) were judged during the Winckelmann epoch and their evaluation in our times, when we have the opportunitiy of comparing them with much earlier works of the grand period. An indirect reflection of the indicated difference (the twofold attitude of aesthetic consciousness) is provided by that radical change in the assessment of an art work when it becomes clear whether it is an original or just a simple copy (a non-independent imitation). This difference also explains that fundamental reevaluation and changing of artistic means each time an older style gives way to a new one. Hence it is clear that the art historian in virtue of his direct relationship to works of art is closer to the creative artist than to the perceiving observer. The moment of free creativity is of greater significance in the artist's or art historian's perception than in that of the ordinary observer.

VII

Let us return, however, to the main question of our investigation. The arguments up to this point had to show and explain why on the way of its inner evolution art history inevitably moves from unconditional evaluation toward a comparative one. The vitality and naturality of this transition is even more evident when we reformulate the question as follows.

The methods determining an artistic composition's structure first of all depend on the sensory material a certain type of art is working with. And in this sensory material there always is a certain variety of aspects or features that await the artist's formative hand. (For example, in the word these are its semantic aspect, emotional quality, syntactic and rhythmic structure, euphony, and so on). Now that which is usually called the richness and contentfulness of artistic form is contingent on how much it uses, i.e., aesthetically transforms, all the possibilities offered by the material being worked on. Therefore this circumstance just is the crucial moment in determining the form's aesthetic value. But because this richness and contentfulness comes in a great variety of degrees, evaluation in such cases inevitably will be comparative and relational in nature. Of course, the judgment must in all cases be teleologically justified, i.e., be based on the artist's purpose, since it is only on the nature of this purpose that the possibility or necessity of using one or another quality of the material depends. And such a use will not always be a stylistic task for the artist. Sometimes the very nature of a style does not permit the aesthetic actualization of this or that possibility and demands that the artist not use it (for example, colors in a drawing or engraving, instrumentation in abstract music, and so on). In such cases, on the basis of the teleological structure of the style (artistic idea), one must decide what it is we have here: an aesthetically justified abstraction or simply a case of artistic impotence and incompetence.

Let us now summarize what has been discussed. We have seen reason to believe that only that type of an art work's analysis that does not content itself with simply stating what the work's decisive factors and elements are but explains their significance to the whole—both the significance of each element taken separately and that of all of them taken together—can be called an aesthetic analysis in the true sense of that word and can be the basis for a scholarly treatment of the art style. Such an analysis, we've seen, inevitably is in the nature of a judgment: its point of departure is an unconditional evaluation, and its result is a comparative and relative valuation. Both of these ways of evaluation derive from the very nature of the aesthetic object, i.e., the teleological structure both of the individual art work and of its style as a totality analyzed as a certain artistic potetiality. To understand this teleological structure, to become aware of its aesthetic significance just is to understand and judge how much the artistic means correspond to the idea embodied with their help, to what degree all the aesthetic possibilities inherent in the sensory are used, what constructive factors have a decisive significance, i.e., perform the function of the dominant, and finally, to what extent the idea itself is embodied within the boundaries of a certain kind of art: this question is crucial in cases where two heterogeneous art forms might be confused or the ways and methods of one art form intrude into those of another (i.e., the problem raised by Lessing's *Laocoön* on the relation between painting and poetry, and so on).

Proceeding from this evaluative moment inherent in the very essence of aesthetic analysis, the history of art can reveal the progressive or regressive development of this or that artistic tendency; affirm the flourishing or decline of an individual artist's or an entire epoch's style; and, finally, on the basis of all these investigations, compare the artistic achievements of various periods, nations, and cultural epochs from the viewpoint of comparative aesthetic judgment. Only one should not forget that in such cases this judgment is immediately directed not to the art work as a whole, but first of all concerns the separate artistic factors and their contribution to the compositional structure as well as their appropriateness to the principal artistic idea. That's why comparative evaluation is applicable only to factors of one kind of artistic significance in works embodying one kind of idea. And only in adding up the results of many such partial comparisons and evaluations does the art historian characterize the conditional aesthetic value of the entire work or the totality of different works belonging to one artist, one school, one epoch, and so on. However, an evaluation of this sort will always be secondary, mediated, derivative, and necessarily dependent on a primary and unmediated evaluation connected with this or that individual artistic factor. For example, the question, Who is the greater artist, Pushkin or Lermontov? lacks, in this general form, strict scholarly meaning, since not only the creative fields of both artists but also their artistic directions are too different and hence cannot be evaluated by the method of comparison. But if the question were, Who of these two is the greater lyric poet? then it could be significant and scientifically justified provided we indicate on which aesthetic factors the comparative evaluation is to be based: the musicalness of the poems, their rhythmic and syntactic structure; their linguistic expressiveness; all of these moments taken together, etc. Likewise in the field of the plastic arts the method of comparison can be evaluatively applied only to one and the same type of artists and art schools, i.e., those who in their work set out to perform the same aesthetic tasks, for example, drawers, colorists, etc. Additionally, it is crucial to bear in mind the significance of that leading factor (dominant) that one or the other artist emphasizes in the totality of his artistic composition; for instance, is the drawing or color-scheme intended only for the benefit of a "formal" beauty, or does its purpose lie primarily in evoking expressivity or the power of emotive impression?

In all these cases the criterion of the comparative evaluation must be provided by the artistic style of the epoch in question. And this means that the crterion must be internal, not external. The evaluation is not limited (as, for example, measuring is) to simple fact-stating as to what is larger or smaller, better or worse; it springs directly from the dynamism of a vital aesthetic consciousness which cannot fail to set itself specific atrtistic tasks and to seek their most perfect fulfillment. One who has understood this thought and looked at it from all sides can have no doubts either about the possibility of comparative evaluation or about its necessity for the stylistic researches of the art historian. Indeed, what can the evolution of art a diligent investigator talks about possibly mean if not (a) progress or regress in solving the artistic problems raised by one or another epoch, in revealing the aesthetic potentialities lying in a certain style, and in organically applying artistic means toward realizing a compositional idea, or (b) the emergence—in times of stylistic change—of new artistic tasks and new ways of handling them, i.e., all that which is caused by a change in artistic taste, manifesting itself in a weakened interest in, and sensitivity to, one sort of artistic moments and a heightened receptivity to others. And how can this newness and originality that an art historian so attentively looks for be ascertained, if not by comparing the artist (or style) being analyzed with all his (or its) predecessors and contemporaries? Finally, how else to characterize the significance of aesthetic originality if not by comparing the artistic means in which it is objectively embodied.[5] In a word, comparative evaluation cannot be disconnected from all those problems of art history that concern the investigation of its principal object, artistic style.

Now that we have apparently gotten clear on the evaluative nature of stylistic analysis in the history of art, we can understand a feature of this discipline that often sounds like an objection to it and is held to show a lack of scholarly strictness and exactitude. If the act of artistic perception and comprehension ir not only the starting point of scholarly analysis but also determines its subsequent direction and progress, then of course the plausibility and comprehensibility of the analysis will depend on whether the author of that analysis is able to indicate the proper way of understanding the art work or style under scrutiny. But an artistic effect can be obtained only with artistic means. That is why the best art historians are not simply archaeologists but real connoisseurs of art who in their stylistic descriptions of paintings and sculptures insensibly turn into poets (like, for example, Heinrich Wölfflin in his works *Classic Art* and *Renaissance and Baroque*). This isn't an entertainment which they take up in their desire to at least partially escape from the depressive discipline of scholarly thinking. No, it is an inescapable methodological means that the investigator avails himself of when he finds no other way to channel scientific analysis in the requisite direction. A truly poetic word is congenial to that immediate impression that a work of art excites no matter what form of art it belongs to.

VIII

However, if the use of poetic means of depiction and description arises from the art historian's commitment to art itself, no less serious are his commitments to science. In whatsoever case his investigation cannot limit itself to picturesque description, for then it would lose its scholarly, methodical significance. In order that the analysis of an art work or style be complete, all the objective content of the aesthetic perception (i.e., all that the poetic description strives to convey) must be translated into a language of accurate scientific concepts adequate to that content. And what are these concepts? Clearly, they are not just theoretical (e.g., logical or psychological) concepts, for if they were, they wouldn't be able to capture what is most important in artistic perception—its value-laden nature. Therefore, they must be aesthetic concepts, i.e., those referring to aesthetic values and moments. But if so, the essential tie between art history and aesthetics becomes evident. The stylistic analysis of a work of art is possible only if it is grounded on those aesthetic concepts, categories, and principles that are set down by aesthetics in its capacity as a science of aesthetic values, of the factors that determine these values, and of their necessary interrelations. In this sense the history of art must be something like applied, special aesthetics.[6] Only thus will art history be able to distinguish itself from archaeology or the history of spiritual and material culture in general and become a history, in the truest sense of that word, of the evolution of art forms and styles. The analysis of style, after all, is now generally acknowledged to be the principal task of art history. But only the grounding of style by the categories of aesthetics can make evident the independence of the problem of style itself and justify its inner unity.

Nevertheless, this kind of orienting of art history toward aesthetics usually provokes the following serious objection: aesthetics, so it is said, is a science as yet so little advanced and so lacking in objective content that basing oneself on it not only will not facilitate and advance the historian's work but, on the contrary, will inevitably make it harder by introducing disputable and scientifically poorly confirmed moments. Thus wouldn't it be better for the history of art to hold on to the status quo, i.e., to remain a purely empirical and descriptive science content with the simple exposition of things encountered in the objective content of art works and avoiding any kind of philosophical explanations and arguments?

But this objection only shows that art historians themselves have not yet attained a sufficiently clear methical awareness of their tasks, that they fail to realize the murky condition in which they find themselves, and that therefore they do not notice how undeveloped and unclarified are the basic concepts on which they are forced to rely in their specific work. Indeed one must only review more closely the methodological inventory of art history to have it become exceedingly clear that the very fundamental concepts with which it operates are undoubtedly concepts of aesthetics (for example, composition, style, rhythm, to name a few). These concepts conceal a certain unity of diversities, a certain synthesis and harmony of interrelated elements; but this unity and this synthesis are very special: they cannot be fully characterized by features from the theoretical vocabulary; their true meaning is disclosed only by an immediate artistic perception and understanding. But if art historians claim that they can do perfectly well without any exposition of the aesthetic meaning of these concepts, it being enough just to hold on to their "objectively" ascertained theoretical content, they are actually deluding themselves and thereby impeding the methical development of art history. In his work the art historian either limits himself to the morphological description of art works and thereby fails to reach the most important object of art history, which is stylistic analysis, or he uses aesthetic concepts unconsciously (analogously to purely theoretical concepts) without scholarly reflection having clarified and fixed their specifically aesthetic property which determines the style's essence. Otherwise put, he uses those concepts in a way that strictly scientifically speaking is illegitimate. Of course, aesthetics itself is still very far from a phenomenological analysis and the settling of the fundamental aesthetic concepts, but it will master this task only in close cooperation with art history, which alone can provide aesthetics with the specific material indispensable for the elucidation of the peculiar nature of aesthetic values.

The alliance with aesthetics will be useful to the historian of art also because it will forever free him from the necessity of using those homemade, scientifically unwarranted aesthetic theories which he has appealed to up to now and which considerably obscure the methodical foundations of art history.

IX

But the grounding of art history in aesthetics does not yet methodically exhaust the issue of judgment connected with the perception and understanding of art. All the types of evaluation we considered concern only the aesthetic object, i.e., what is usually called artistic form. But in works of art we value not just the pure form; judgment can also be passed on those meanings and values that characterize the material worked on independently of its artistic form. Thus, for example, all kinds of narrative and representational (object-related) art require attention also to what they characteristically express, i.e., to what is customarily held to be the art work's meaning or content. In other words, the perceiver's attention is naturally and inevitably drawn to those cultural phenomena and the values (moral, religious, social, etc.) embodied in them that supplied the art work with its material and dictated its theme or subject. Even when considering works of non-objective art (e.g., music), we talk about their profundity, the importance of their emotional content. And even though this material moment (the content moment) is embraced by the form, even though the creative activity of the artist transforms this moment into a formally higher principle; still, it cannot be judged merely from the formal viewpoint, but requires to be judged from its own point of view on its own merits. This requirement is what raises the question of what this or that artist or style added to the cultural heritage of humanity and the question of how much the art of a certain epoch succeeded in expressing the fundamental values and essential spiritual aspirations of its age. An answer to these questions will contain a judgment on the significance of a work's or style's content as well as on the depth and breadth of its historical influence. But such a judgment, as we saw, is not an aesthetic evaluation in the strict sense of the word. Rather, it concerns culture generally, since it inquires about the significance of art and its creations for culture as a whole. Even so it does not remain beyond the bounds of artistic perception and comprehension but in a certain peculiar way aligns itself to them. This can be explained by what makes an aesthetic object's structure special. This object does not exist by itself but always presupposes an objectivity of another sort out of which it arises. Moreover, this pre-aesthetic objective foundation is not left wholly outside the boundary of the aesthetic object, although the latter does not totally absorb it, either. It retains its nature, as if shining through the artistic form embodying it. Therefore, almost every work of art has accumulated within it not only aesthetic but also non-aesthetic values (moral, cognitive, etc.) and has to be judged accordingly. This non-aesthetic valuation, however, is not independent (otherwise it wouldn't enter into the make-up of an aesthetic perception), but is connected with aesthetic judgment and is made possible by it. In other words, a work of art not only embodies beauty (aesthetic values) but also expresses in that beauty—or, to use Plato's words, gives birth to—other, non-aesthetic values. In methodological terms this means that non-aesthetic valuation necessarily depends on a formal aesthetic judgment; otherwise the valuation would lose its internal justification, i.e., it would not be the evaluation of an *art* work, hence, it would not be organically connected with an immediate artistic perception.

In this structural feature of artistic perception whereby it includes non-aesthetic evaluation as well, there resides an effective power of that (organic) life force that unites art with all other areas of culture. This connection, needless to say, is neither accidental nor unimportant for art, for it determines its role and significance for culture as a whole. As a manifestation of a unified cultural totality, art can be judged only from the viewpoint of the spiritual content revealing itself in it, of the cultural values that its artistic form embodies. Not just general aesthetics, but also the aesthetics of individual kinds of art cannot avoid raising this problem. But looking at it from the viewpoint of scientific methodology, this is a final, limiting issue that arises when the question of the unity of cultural creativity comes up, a question about that common ground in which the multiplicity of all cultural forces and values thrives. If one wishes to understand this common ground correctly, one must first have a full and clear view of the peculiar and independent nature of art. Otherwise aesthetics and with it the history of art will again be subjected to that fateful error that for a long time made their activities fruitless and unproductive. That error is the mixing together of questions pertaining to the core of art with those pertaining to the importance of art for culture.

X

The main task of our investigation is now completed. We have explained in what sense aesthetic evaluation is an inseparable factor in the stylistic analysis of works of art and how this evaluative attitude towards the object analyzed, an attitude mandatory for the art historian, can be scientifically justified and confirmed only on the basis of aesthetics. The alliance of art history and aesthetics that we've sketched is, of course, no more than a program that has yet to be implemented. And only when it has begun to be carried out *in concreto*, will all the difficulties and complications lurking in it perhaps become apparent. Some of these difficulties may be envisaged ahead of time, for in the schematic form in which we've presented the essentials of our program it lacks unambiguous definition and might easily be wrongly expanded upon. To the extent possible, let us try to forestall some such expansions. For example, we cannot quietly circumvent those fears that the method of evaluation usually engenders in art historians: its application to stylistic analysis is allegedly equivalent to an acknowledgment that aesthetics determines artistic taste, that it can incorrigibly decide what is beautiful and what is not, and that it can define obligatory norms regulating all creative endeavors. Such a conception of aesthetics and the evaluation associated with it is, of course, wholly mistaken; but holding it to be so in no way threatens the conclusions of our investigation. For aesthetics, as contemporary philosophy understands it, creates neither an aesthetic experience nor the aesthetic judgment that this experience harbors, though it provides for the one and the other as certain factual data. The problem of aesthetics is only to reveal and record in the language of concepts what is contained that experience and what constitutes its necessary constitutive factors. A general canon obligatory both for all artistic creativity and for each work individually is not something that aesthetics either can or should set.

As a completed independent totality, every work of art is autonomous, as if it were governed by an individual principle all its own, a principle giving it a special inner necessity and fusing into a unity all the structural elements that make it up. Hence, a unified and universal ideal of beauty, as venerated in the 18th century, just doesn't exist. There are as many aesthetic ideals as there are epochs and styles of art. But to recognize that the most diverse artistic aspirations can from the aesthetic viewpoint be equally valid is not at all to deny the existence of objective aesthetic criteria nor to affirm an extreme aesthetic relativism according to which beauty is a relative thing and the significance and power of all concrete manifestations of beauty depend only on a certain epoch and on a certain artistic taste. Consistently maintaining this view would require abjuring any kind of comparative valuation. On that view an art work can only be perceived and judged as absolutely closed and inimitable in its individuality; therefore, it is utterly incomparable with anything else. If we accept this conclusion, then clearly the unconditional judgment connected with artistic perception will be a completely irrational fact that cannot be investigated scientifically.[7] In other words, in that case art history as a science would become impossible. But the blandishments of this type of scepticism are not as dangerous for scientific thought as might at first glance appear. Not only is scepticism fruitless; it is quite incompatible with the data of scientific experience.

Despite all its imperfections, the history of art is no illusion but an undeniable fact which for its justification requires no more than an explanation of the conditions that determine it. And this we have already done. Artistic perception, of course, cannot immediately become scientific knowledge: with respect to the latter the former always remains transcendental. But its content, as we have seen, can be translated into the language of scientific concepts. Since in any case of translation the original is somewhat changed, such a change also happens to the artistic perception when it becomes an object of scholarly reflection. Breaking in that reflection like a ray of sun breaks in a prism, it fragments into its structural elements. This the task of scholarly investigation is not only to describe these elements but also to determine their inner connection as the cause of the artistic composition's unity. This connection as well as the moments determining it have, as we've clarified, a teleological nature. That's why the stylistic analysis is essentially intentional, inevitably directed toward the totality of the artistic composition even though it never fully realizes it within itself. In this way the unity of artistic perception is not only the stylistic investigation's starting point but also its conclusion (that which it must recreate); both of these limit points are already beyond the boundaries of scientific reflection. In this way there follows one particularly important conclusion about the object of art history. The internal (immanent) object of scientific reflection (i.e., the object it not only has in mind but in which it actually exists) is not the work of art as a complete whole but the individual compositional elements and their determinant inner (teleological) directedness with respect to the whole (their relation to the totality). Comparing these objective data the history of art brings to light the general nature of both the structural factors and their characteristic teleological tendencies and thus recreates that aesthetic potentiality that determines the style of individual art works. Hence the true object of art history is nothing other than a certain *relation* between aesthetic potentiality and individual artistic creations, which are analyzed from the point of view of the embodiment of the former (i.e., the potentiality) in the latter (i.e., the creations). And it is important that a total coincidence of the potentiality with its specific actualization is impossible. Even if we take the concept of potentiality as narrowly as possible (as the potentiality not of an entire epoch but of a single artist or even just one of his creative periods), that potentiality will always be relatively general with the possibility of receiving quite various embodiments. But this cannot be otherwise, since only a conception of art history that requires that individual art phenomena be analyzed in their relation to something general is what makes it possible for this discipline, and for the comparative aesthetic evaluation associated with it, to be a science. If there were no concept of aesthetic potentiality, in respect of which we analyze individual art works, there wouldn't be their common denominator which makes possible their comparative evaluation and which grounds the scientific objectivity of that evaluation. For the criteria of evaluation directly follow from the creative tendencies that describe aesthetic potentiality. For example, some tendencies are of crucial importance; they are so general that they are equally important for all areas of artistic creativity. Take the aspiration, characteristic of all kinds of art, completely to dissolve the worked-on sensory material in artistic form, that is, aesthetically to use all its facets and qualities. In each art form this tendency acquires this or that individualized expression and in this way not only reveals the positive possibilities of that art form but also sets it certain limits that it cannot transgress.

For artistic creativity and its tendencies no less important than the structure of the sensory material worked on are the conditions related to the nature of artistic perception. These conditions depend on the perceiving subject; therefore, we can call them subjective and psychological in the usual sense. But phenomenologically speaking, from the viewpoint of the aesthetic object's reality, they are no less objective than the conditions inherent in the sensory nature of the material. A prime example is the already indicated feature of artistic perception whereby one compositional factor is always of crucial significance and plays the part of a unifying (organizing) dominant. But in a specific case of its realization this dominant may correspond to a very different concept of it. The compositional factors of an art work are so heterogeneous in their nature and significance, and the degrees of their independence or of their mutual relations of dependence are so diverse, that not all of them can become dominants equally or in the same sense. Therefore aesthetic value is possessed not by every synthesis of compositional elements joined by this or that dominant but only by that synthesis that emphasizing in a special manner certain facets of the material worked on or revealing a peculiar way of perceiving them gives all of these structural factors an independent, contemplation-inducing value (significance). Which types of synthesis of aesthetically significant compositional elements are possible in general and what dominants determine these, are questions hitherto very little investigated. A separate inquiry is needed for each type of art here. And doubtless from this specific aesthetics the history of art will gather many hints that will help it to give meaning to, and to justify aesthetically, its own formal (morphological) analysis of art works.[8]

All of the conditions indicated (both those connected with the structure of the material worked on and those flowing from the nature of the perceiving subject) bring artistic creativity under the influence of a certain regularity, i.e., direct it into a certain groove or rather system of grooves in which the process of its growth, development, and decline takes place. These same conditions also determine the direction of possible artistic tendencies and thus are an objective foundation of that comparative (relative) evaluation that is the task of art history's stylistic analysis. Thus it is clear that this judgment is not based on some obscure absolute ideal of art that is universal for all times and all nations; but, on the other hand, neither is it dependent on subjective arbitrariness or inconstant and changing historical circumstances. No, it is firmly rooted in those objective possibilities in the sphere of which the real historical life of artistic creativity takes place.

XI

The most important reason why we devoted this essay to analyzing the issue of evaluation in the history of art is that we think that one or another solution of it is of decisive import to the correct understanding of the methods and tasks of this science. Only upon grasping its system-related foundations and having accurately clarified its object's nature can art history justify the specific features of its characteristic methods and free itself from the shackles of a thinking peculiar to the natural sciences, a thinking that still influences many of the humanities. For value judgments are held to be inadmissible in art history precisely because they are entirely lacking in the natural sciences and mathematics, i.e., those disciplines characterized by accuracy and logical consistency. In other words, the way of thinking peculiar to mathematics and natural science is held to be the ideal of science in general, totally forgetting that the methods of any science are first of all determined by the nature of the object it investigates and that therefore one cannot mechanically transfer the methods of one science to the field of another. What characterizes the mechanistic and mathematical thinking prevalent in the natural sciences is that it depersonalizes the objects it investigates, i.e. it does research on them in abstraction of their specific meaning and significance. Clearly, such scientific ways and methods are inappropriate when cognition is presented with the task of revealing and grasping that *special* significance of the object under scrutiny. Therefore all attempts in the history of art to base oneself on the natural sciences and to orient oneself to their methods are bound to fail. Furthermore, such attempts direct this science onto the wrong path and distort its true significance. But art history can unfold this significance and be guided by it in all its researches only if it enters into a close relationship with that discipline that it up to now avoided, not having received from it the methodic help it needed. The rapprochment of art history and aesthetics is one of the most pressing tesks of scientific methodology, the successful performance of which will be equally beneficial to both sciences.

Endnotes

1   In criticizing Taine's theory, Ernst Grosse (in his book *The Beginnings of Art*) correctly argues that the explanations Taine offers for the historical origin of various art forms and art styles are incomplete: Taine notes only the coincidence of these forms and styles with this or that natural social milieu but doesn't look for any causal dependence of the former on the latter.
2   Of course, from the point of view not of some abstract ideal, but of those specific stylistic objectives that it tries to achieve.
3   Because of the confusion of these aesthetic mindsets the understanding of aesthetic contemplation is often murky and inaccurate.
4   That is why geometric figures not harmonized with a variation of form have no aesthetic significance (i.e., a circle, a square).
5   In judging an art work's originality, we first of all emphasize not the newness of the means used but the increasing number and variety of aesthetic values actualized by that work. Even though the differential sensations by which originality is determined help form the aesthetic impression they do not create it by themselves. They are necessary for picking out and highlighting the phenomenon but they are not sufficient for making it an independently, hence also aesthetically, valuable object. Differential sensations can also be aesthetically negative; for example, they arise when stylistic canons are violated. The originality of a language by no means guarantees its artistic value.
6   This thought, among others, was raised by Heinrich Wölfflin in the foreword to his capital treatise *Classic Art*. He is perhaps the sole famous contemporary art historian who grasped the necessity of conjoining art history with aesthetics and who on the basis of this understanding carried out his scholarly research.: in addition to analyzing both individual works of art and whole groups of them, he devotes some sections of his work to drawing general aesthetic judgments and to determining the aesthetic significance of the phenomena discussed.
7   Scientific analysis is inseparably tied to comparative reflection, and the comparison of value-related phenomena inevitably issues in comparative evaluation.
8   Of course, this doesn't mean that this specific aesthetics will instruct artists as to what paths they should pursue. Only an immediate artistic perception can declare one or another compositonal form as having genuine artistic value. And it is the task of aesthetics to reveal those objective conditions that determine the worth of a specific form and thereby to justify the aesthetic tendency underlying it.

AESTHETICS

Aesthetics (Greek: αισθητική (*aisthetike*)) is the science that elucidates the nature and essence of aesthetic values. These values—beauty and its relatives (nobility, tragicality, comicality)—are distinguished by the fact (1) that they are perceived only in things or phenomena that are in one or another way accessible to the senses (primarily vision and hearing) and the fact (2) that the perceptual act itself is not purely theoretical but also emotive, i.e., connected with a certain emotional reaction on the part of the perceiving subject. This reaction is disinterested, i.e., the aesthetic object is evaluated independently of its practical significance for the subject. The aesthetic experience has both an objective and a subjective moment. On the one hand, there is the nature and structure of the perceived object which is aesthetically evaluated; on the other, there is the perceptual act and the associated emotional condition of the subject (delighting in the object). The act of perception is based on a special "contemplative" mental attitude; and it is only to this attitude or mindset that aesthetic values are accessible. Aesthetics is one of the principal disciplines of the system of philosophy, for aesthetic values are independent and cannot be directly derived from any other values. It is the foundation of the general theory of art.

As an independent science aesthetics appeared much later than the other main disciplines of philosophy (logic, ethics, gnoseology, philosophy of nature). At first philosophers discussing the problem of beauty turned their attention less to to the peculiar nature of beauty than to its significance for one or another area of life and identified it with other values. The Sophists reduced beauty to utility, purposiveness, or pleasure, and thought it was relative. Plato overcame the relativism of the Sophists by deriving the beauty of things from the idea of beauty, which idea being a supersensory entity coincided in its content with the idea of goodness and thereby with real being (truth). It provided the basis for the harmony of the physical and spiritual world. From Plato onwards this three-sided unity (goodness-beauty-truth) played a highly significant methodological part (especially in Neoplatonism). Plato authored the rational aesthetics that holds beauty to be an object of pure thought. Aristotle, like Plato, conceived aesthetic appreciation in rationalist terms. Medieval philosophy added nothing essentially new to Plato's and Aristotle's conceptions. Only after the Renaissance did certain new aesthetic currents appear; even though they held on to tradition they, by expanding one or another of its motifs, prepared the ground for the emergence of an independent aesthetics.

The *Rationalist aesthetics* in 17th and 18th century France and Germany recognized as aesthetically valuable only that which met the demands of reason. Thence arises the formula of Nicolas Boileau: "Only that is beautiful which is true." Clarity and rationality are the sole criteria for aesthetic taste. According to Gottfried Wilhem Leibniz and his successors Christian Wolff and Alexander Baumgarten, the object of aesthetic knowledge is cosmic harmony and meaningful lawlikeness; aesthetic knowledge differs from theoretical (scientific) knowledge in that the former is based not on thought but on sense-experience, which is an inferior grade of knowing (*gnoseologia inferior*) that has not reached the perfect clarity accessible only to thinking. Baumgarten, who expanded and systematized these ideas of Leibniz, became famous in the Age of Enlightenment also for coining the name "aesthetics" and giving the subject a special place in the system of philosophy.

English aesthetics in the 17th and 18th centuries turned radically away from Platonic and Aristotelian rationalism and was first of all interested in the subjective and emotive side of aesthetic impressions. In keeping with the empiricist method it sought not so much to explain aesthetic facts as to describe them accurately. The most important conclusions of Lord Shaftesbury, Francis Hutcheson and David Hume were as follows: (1) aesthetic impressions necessarily contain a certain emotive quality that depends, among other things, on their close tie to organic feelings; (2) although this emotive nature distinguishes them from cognitive acts yet aesthetic impressions are not to be identified with simple (egoistic) emotions nor with the moral sense, even though they are akin to the latter in that they are disinterested and do not issue in volitional or instinctual activity; and (3) the aesthetic sense must be recognized as an independent and original faculty of the mind which cannot be derived from other mental phenomena or abilities.

A decisive turning point in the history of aesthetics came with the the *theory of beauty* proposed by *Immanuel Kant*. On the one hand, this theory brings out those factors that determine the independence and intrinsic value of the aesthetic object; on the other, it emphasizes the special character of aesthetic consciousness, as constituted by the these facts: (1) aesthetic satisfaction is "disinterested"; in this it differs from the feeling of pleasure and all positive moral emotions; (2) an aesthetic judgment, like a theoretical one, is characterized by universality and necessity; however, unlike the latter it is not founded on general concepts but (3) immediately perceives and appreciates the object's teleological (purposive) structure, in which, just like in an organism, the goal corresponds to the means that realize it, i.e., to the concrete and finished unity of its incarnation (form). This free, or formal, beauty is distinguished by Kant from beauty dependent on the object's content; thus his aesthetics splits into two parts: the aesthetics of pure (sensory) form and the aesthetics of objective content.

In order to eschew this dualism, some of Kant's successors confine the aesthetic sphere to pure form and remove from aesthetics whatever cannot be deduced from the object's formal order. This formalist position was championed by Johann Friedrich Herbart and his disciples: beauty, in their opinion, is determined by the relations between the object's parts or elements. Others, by contrast, assign a decisive role to the objective significance (content, idea) and regard the sensory form as but a vehicle for the embodiment of that significance, a vehicle that is valuable only insofar as it expresses that content. This view is held by all the *idealist philosophers* (Friedrich Wilhem Schelling, Georg Wilhelm Friedrich Hegel, Arthur Schopenhauer), the Romanticists, and later Hermann Lotze. Their aesthetic views exhibit a constructive nature; they attempt to derive beauty from that metaphysical (unconditional) element which provides their system's foundation (the Absolute, Divine Spirit, Cosmic Will, and the like).

In the second half of the 19th century there arose, in reaction to these a priori metaphysical constructions, a *positivist and empiricist aesthetics*. Its founder Gustav Theodor Fechner insisted that a scientific aesthetics had to be constructed not from above but from below; i. e., on the basis of observations and experiments. Aesthetics should be treated as a special branch of empirical psychology.

The aesthetic theories of our day are distinguished mainly by what they appeal to in the way of laying down aesthetic principles. One can appeal to (1) the aesthetic impression (the experience of the perceiving subject); or to (2) the aesthetic object (the work of art, the beauty of nature); or, since it is the human being himself who creates aesthetic objects (works of art), to (3) the creative act (the spiritual attitude and activity of the creative artist). Aesthetics has to avail itself of all three ways, but its main point of view depends on which of these moments is held to be the most significant. The first and the third method emphasize the subject's role, thus usually leading to a subjectivist justification of aesthetics. The second is usually associated wih an objectivist conception of aesthetics. The first road, for example, is traversed by the empathy theory and kindred conceptions (Theodor Lipps, Johannes Volkelt, and others). The second is held to by those theories that derive art from man's instinct to be creatively active and that hold beauty to be a perfect expression of the emotive state caused in the subject by one or another impression (Karl Groos, Benedetto Croce, and others). Finally, the third methodical road is travelled by those aestheticians who explain aesthetic values and the subject's emotional reaction to them by the sensory structure of the art object itself (A. von Hildebrandt, Heinrich Wölfflin, Henri Focillon, Raymond Bayer, and others). A separate niche is occupied by phenomenological aesthetics, which in analyzing aesthetic phenomena and experiences attempts to highlight their common ideal essence and meaning (Moritz Geiger).

AESTHETIC CULTURE AND AESTHETIC EDUCATION

In our times the problem of aesthetic culture takes on an ever greater significance. Art is neither game-plating nor something entertaining nor an adornment of life but the most serious duty of the human spirit. Its importance is not limited to serving as a powerful means of moral education; it also has an independent value, and the less it submits to incidental concerns foreign to it, the greater its influence. Consequently, no culture can fully express its essence and open up all the possibilities inherent in it if does not also participate in the creation of art.

All these principles have such a currency in our contemporary consciousness that no one anywhere seriously contradicts them. But it is just now that aesthetic culture encounters the most serious obstacles in its development. What is more, there are a number of signs showing that its very existence is in danger. There are, of course, various reasons for this; but the most important ones lie in the very nature of our contemporary culture.

In fact, the most conspicuous feature of that culture is its extremely fast growth in width, hugely surpassing its growth in depth. The culture of our time is essentially democratic, taking in ever broader layers of the populace. At the same time it is extremely complex in its internal structure, in the variety of the fields that enter into it: for example, the sciences, the arts, civic life, and so on. Thus an individual person cannot take in all of culture, cannot perceive and experience it fully in all its various manifestations. He can grasp it only within the limits that are set for him by his profession, his social position, and his life environment. He knows all other fields and aspects of culture superficially from books, newspapers, lectures, the opinions of other people, and so on. . . . Now it is that broad layer of half-cultured people that becomes important; for they, as Socrates observed, pose a greater threat to the development of culture than do utterly uneducated people and outright barbarians. These half-educated persons deem themselves to be the champions of true enlightenment, although having but a superficial grasp of culture they neither see nor understand its real spiritual essence. The deadly fruits of this bastardization of culture are evident everywhere, but they're particularly striking in the sphere of aesthetic culture. True creativity is replaced by mechanical imitation; the artistic imagination weakens, hiding its feebleness under a glare of outward effects.

Things of this sort have occurred before, of course; in our times they've become huge and dangerous. We often hear it said that democratic culture is in principle impossible, that culture is essentially aristocratic, and that it has always been and will be the prerogative of a choice minority. This claim is, of course, wrong; it is correct only in the sense that individual creative powers are always concentrated in a minority of people. But this doesn't mean that the masses cannot understand culture at all or take active part in its development. The proof of this lies in the fact of artistic folk creativity. Folk arts constitute not only the initial stage in the historical development of art; they also are that inexhaustible living resource out of which individual creativity draws ever new strength. This was already understood in antiquity. It is no accident that the creators of our great classical culture acknowledged having feasted on the crumbs that fell from Homer's table (i.e., the folk epos). The same can be seen in our times. The development of modern art does not at all show it moving further and further away from the simplicity and elementariness of folk art. On the contrary, art is continuously renouncing its intricate, complex forms and is coming back to the original folk art patterns. This return does not portend any arrest or regress in art; it only means that it has changed direction and has found new, as yet untried possibilities of artistic creation.

But even if there can be no principled objection to democratic culture, the general direction of contemporary spiritual life harbors a great danger to that very life, especially its aesthetic side. Indeed, right in front of our eyes folk culture is slowly but surely dying; many of its branches have withered forever, and only the efforts of collectors and researchers allow a part of it to be saved from total oblivion. The culture of the industrial city overpowers and destroys that of the village and countryside. Since industry, aided by an expanding technology, obliterates more and more of the existing national differences and traits, the culture associated with it acquires increasingly international features. In place of sundry national vestments we get uniform types of European bourgeois suit. Folk dances and games are pushed out by new dances without a homeland. Folk crafts cede their place to factory artifacts suiting the taste of the average European.

This threat of cultural annihilation is already sufficiently clear. The awakening nations of Europe are looking for ways to counter this fading and decaying of aesthetic culture. The biggest weapon here is, of course, education. In the pedagogical literature of the West these last 20 to 25 years the problem of aesthetic education has been one of the most ardently discussed. Some progress has been made. But in general, aesthetic education, even in Europe's most progressive countries, is still in its infancy. In this article we will mention only some points that, in our view, are most important.

The supreme goal of aesthetic education and training is, of course, to ensure that the pupil not only be able to create art but also to understand it. To this end it is not enough to give him broad and detailed facts about this or that field of art. For example, introducing into the school curriculum such things as painting, music history, and so on, only serves to overload the memory capacities of pupils; with the result that one gets back, as experience shown, quite contrary results, i.e., just a purely mechanical rote-learning of the presented material, without any accompanying grasp of art. The disinterest that young people often show in the literary classics from their grammar school years rather clearly indicates, it seems, that we shouldn't go further along this road. As pedagogical experience suggests, to narrow the compass of the obligatory material to be learned is more to the purpose than to broaden it. But that, of course, is not the crux. What is most important is that the teaching material and methods be as much as possible adapted to those abilities to create and understand art that are present in a child's soul. Of course, the execution of this task is connected with great difficulties, but constant and persistent effort in this field can secure the success of aesthetic education. A teacher who likes this sort of work can see very great and tempting perspectives opening up before him.

Indeed, it has long been observed—and the newest scientific research confirms this—that a child's psyche is in many respects akin to the soul of primeval man. That's why children grasp so well the simple and simply perfect forms of folk art. A folk tale with its marvellous fantasy and simple wisdom; a folk song's happy joy and heavy sorrow; the bright variety of folk rituals, games, and dances—all this carries special enchantment for the child; all this settles deeply into his soul, striking a kindred chord. This then opens up a thankful task for aesthetic education: to renew the connection between art's past and present, and not only to safeguard folk creations from oblivion but also to allow them to exercise deep and direct influence on the artistic creativity of the present and the future. To be sure, such an educative effect of folk culture will be possible only if it comes not only from books but presents itself to the generation growing up in all its actual vitality. A folk tale really has to be a live telling in words; and songs, dances, and rituals have to be a current happening in which the child himself takes part and fulfills his aesthetic needs. A great educational advantage of folk art lies in the fact that because of its simplicity it does not subjugate a child's reason and sensibility, does not overwhelm his individual quests and efforts, but on the contrary, awakens and brings to maturity his own creative powers. We should remember that in antiquity, during the period of the greatest flourishing of classical art, elementary education in the public schools of Ellada consisted largely of the Homerian epos and its recitation to the musical accompaniment provided by the pupils themselves.

Primitive art characteristically conjoined in its creations such forms as during the later phases of art's evolution became independent. This was the case for music. Folk art knows no music other than singing and dancing. This circumstance can also be used for aesthetic education. Particularly important in this respect are dances, i.e., rhythmic and rhythmically expressive motions. The example of antiquity is instructive here, too. In rhythm there is to be discerned and valued a great means of education. Rhythm is an element of organization that makes our movements obey a rational and purposive order and thereby makes our bodies a tool obedient to our will and spirit. That is why in antiquity eurhythmy, allowing a harmony of soul and body to manifest itself, was regarded as the most important characteristic—not only internal, but external—of a proper education. In recent years a serious interest in the educational significance of rhythm once again re-emerged in an effort to resuscitate the forgotten traditions of old. It is this goal that the rhthmic gymnastics of Émile Jaques-Dalcroze pursues. But it seeks even more: it attempts to embody in movements not just the rhythm of music but also the inner emotional content of music associated with that rhythm, i.e., it strives to solve a purely art-related problem. Rhythmic gymnastics is of special importance for aesthetic education. There is no other creative act that would involve the whole of man's body and soul in the way that music does when it is turned into rhythmically expressed movements. The results already achieved by rhythmic gymnastics (for instance, its influence on the reform of theater and ballet arts) fully justified the hopes put in it.

The situation is somewhat different with the plastic arts, i.e., painting and sculpture. Acquainting school students and the general public with the works of the great masters of the past can, of course, be of some benefit to aesthetic education. But this is only to begin with. Developing the ability to perceive the forms and colors of the surrounding world with the eye requires an active learning on the part of the students themselves to depict that which they see, i.e., it requires their learning to draw, mold, and paint. In general, the educative significance of these processes is beyond dispute in pedagogics. But aesthetic education is determined by the goal that contemporary teaching sets itself. That goal must not be the reaching of some finished examples giving the pupil a complete schema of visible perceptions. What is most important and, of course, most difficult, is to teach him really to see things (and not just to imagine he sees them) and to depict what he sees on paper or on canvas in the equivalent language of lines, colors, shadows, etc. The variety of plastic art styles in different nations at different periods emerges in accordance with how these nations or periods perceive the surrounding world and what in the visible image of that world appears most important and dear to them. The more sensitive an eye is to the variety of nature's visible forms, the broader is the array of the creative possibilities opening up to it and the better and more lively is its feeling for style. In this sense nature truly is the only teacher of a painter or sculptor, for to investigate nature is not to copy it in a servile way, but creatively to rebuild it. And only by investigating nature can one really understand the forms of style created on by-gone times and their artistic significance.

In conclusion we shall add that even contemporary media must as much as possible be used for aesthetic culture. If, for example, the cinema is already successfully being used for general education and especially scientific purposes, then it can play no less of a role in aesthetic education. It is no accident that the cinematic technique gave rise to a new and highly promising type of art: so-called "dynamic painting."

Of course, with respect to the democratization of aesthetic culture one should not harbor optimistic illusions. As long as aesthetic education subjects are just incidental addenda to the general school curriculum, rather than being organically connected with it, this issue is irresolvable. It can be solved only when the entire system of education is filled with a spirit suitable for the main purposes of aesthetic culture.

PHYSICAL EDUCATION AND AESTHETIC CULTURE

In the ideal state, according to Plato, two things must be put at the foundation of citizens' education: gymnastics and music. They are the basis upon which the entire subsequent fostering of mind and character must be built. And that further fostering must bring to maturity and let flourish whatever has been implanted in the pupil at that initial stage. Thus gymnastics and music are reckoned by Plato to be the fittest means to implement *kalokagathia*, i.e., that harmony of psychical and bodily forces (abilities) from which there arise and in which there spread out all intellectual and moral virtues. It is quite important to remark that Plato, in delineating his system of education, does not yield to that ascetic idealism that so clearly asserts itself in some of his works, for example, the *Phaedo*; i.e., he does not regard body and soul as incompatible items standing in each other's way but, on the contrary, he holds their continuous and harmonious interaction to be a necessary and essential condition for human thriving. What is more, Plato does not represent this interaction as a relationship between two distinct elements that grow and develop equivalently and self-sufficiently. Priority in this process of human development is accorded not to the difference between body and soul, but to their *unity*. They first of all constitute an *organic whole*; and only within the limits of this totality can there occur a differentiation of physical and mental abilities. That is why a genuine physical education also fosters the soul.

On the other hand, mental abilities can be educated and strengthened only by awakening and encouraging the physical capabilities of the organism. Not only the soul, but the body also must be rational, i.e., be able to accommodate to those functions that it must fulfill. For the soul, too, the mind's intellectual penetration and inventiveness are not enough; it needs willpower, energy, and the power to resist—i.e., all that on which the organic power of the body, its vitality, is founded. Thus Plato does not view gymnastics and music as teaching aids geared to entirely distinct fields of education—so that gymnastics would be intended for exercising the body, and music would serve to ennoble the soul. Rather, gymnastics and music together must shape and fashion the whole psychophysical organism. The only difference is that the task of gymnastics is to develop and strengthen the natural activity of the organism, while music provides it with the essentials of measure and harmony; i.e., it hones the organism's ability to use its energy purposefully and to give its manifestations the most fitting and best form.

The pedagogy of modern times, even though it constantly repeated the ancient formula *mens sana in corpore sano*, did not succeed in ridding itself of the dualistic view that became predominant in the Middle Ages. This educational theory succumbed to an intellectualist way of thinking; it radically separated spiritual (mental) and physical education, regarding the latter as secondary. A decisive change of mind occurred only at the beginning of the 20th century, when there arose a mighty reaction to the one-sided intellectualism of European culture, and sports gained an influential and honorable position in European cultural life. We began to appreciate the *kalokagathia* ideal of the ancient Greeks since we understand and recognize the inner connection that the body has with man's spiritual nature and the absolute, irreplaceable value of this connection to the whole of life. Still, this does not mean that we have returned to those views on education that prevailed in Plato's time and that we're attempting to bring back what was created two thousand years ago. History doesn't repeat itself, and every epoch inevitably brings its own problems which have to be solved taking into account the particular demands of the actual moment. For us the *kalokagathia* of antiquity cannot be an absolute and unchanging norm. It should be applied to the present only to the extent of pointing the way in quest of a harmonious unity of body and soul. Our task is, first, to weed out whatever in the ancient viewpoint of *kalokagathia* is no longer compatible with the structure and spirit of contemporary culture and second, to disseminate and expand the supraempirical elements in that viewpoint using all the information we can obtain from the psychology and physiology of our times and from our historical experience.

The ideal of *kalokagathia* was, like almost all ideals of the past, strictly aristocratic in nature. It encompassed all those moral and physical values in virtue of which a true aristocrat differed from an ordinary person. In our age such a conception of *kalokagathia* is unacceptable. This ideal doesn't belong to just one cutural epoch and doesn't constitute an exceptional privilege for a certain class. It is based on the very essence and nature of being human and thus has universal significance. To be sure, it may be deemed an aristocratic ideal insofar as it requires that a human being strive for both bodily and spiritual perfection. But its being aristocratic this way is not at all incompatible with its universality and democratic character; on the contrary, all these things are closely tied together.

In one respect, however, *kalokagathia* is particularly congenial to the spirit of our times, even though this is the case in a quite peculiar way. This becomes clear when we call to mind the exceedingly important part played in our current *Weltaanschauung* by the principle of motion or *movement*. Not only in the natural sciences is this the main principle for explaining all phenomena; in cultural life as well it is accorded an independent significance and value. The *Weltaanschauung* of the ancient world was essentially static. Changeless being was valued higher than becoming.

Movement was looked at as a transitional state, as a way leading to an unmovable and unchangeable goal. Dynamics was under the rule of statics. In modern times the opposite point of view gained ascendancy. *Becoming*, or dynamics, became the dominant factor. The role of constant (unchanging) being was limited to having its "constants" determine the general direction and regularity of becoming (movement). In the 20th century this dynamics attained its highest degree—not only because the tempo of cultural life as a whole considerably quickened but especially because people nowadays are particularly sensitive to any and all manifestations of dynamism. This can be seen in both technology (material culture) and art. The exceptional success and popularity of the cinema stem first of all from the fact that in a film the artistic depiction's center of gravity lies in movements, i.e., in expressive gestures, whereas the role of words, even in talking pictures, is secondary. We might even say that in a movie the word itself becomes an expressive gesture. In this respect, interestingly enough, cinematography had an impact on theater arts. The newest currents here strongly emphasize the dramatic significance of motions and strive to introduce as much movement as possible into the presentations. Finally, there is one more noteworthy feature of our age: this is the flourishing of *choreography* as a unique independent form of art that is increasingly liberating itself from the conditionality and artificiality of traditional ballet and attempts to avail itself of all the possibilities inherent in the nature of the human body.

But the latter example throws light on the contemporary aesthetic tendency from yet another important side. The human being of our times is not only particularly sensitive to the values that manifest themselves in visible motion; he also highly values motion as an elemental expression of a vitality that enables him directly to perceive and to experience the kinship of his body to organic nature as a whole. He is not content with just aesthetically appreciating organic movements; he desires to feel immediately their dynamism and to realize it in his own body. But a body is able to realize its aesthetic potentialities only to the extent that it is strong and disciplined; i.e., its natural forces are trained and can freely assert themselves. In this way the aesthetic culture that people nowadays are most concerned with must be based on physical (bodily) culture or, otherwise put, it must follow the path indicated by Plato and establish an intimate connection between gymnastics and music. In truth, what does Plato's thesis mean on closer inspection?

Each bodily motion takes place in time and space and demands a certain flexing of the muscles. In other words, space (the path), time, and force are those principal moments on which the structure and changes of a motion depend. Depending on its purpose, a motion can be faster or slower, agitated or calm, smooth or jerky, it can occur on a straight or crooked trajectory; but whatever the case it will be purposive and efficient, i.e., achieve the maximum goal with a minimum of expenditure only if there is strictly determinate relationship between its force, its duration, and its path. And the relationship between these moments gives each (purposive) motion a certain special rhythm and dynamics (increase or decrease of tension). The rythmic and dynamic nature of motion becomes clearer still when considering not just an individual elementary motion but those combinations of various motions in which the activity and functioning of the whole body can manifest themselves. In this case what's important is not only that the speed, force, and the bodily inertia of every motion be properly used but also that all the motions be harmonious so that each part of the body can freely do what it is supposed to do. In a word, the bodily discipline on which any kind of sport (running, jumping, swimming, throwing, and so on) is based manages and regulates the rhythm and dynamics of bodily motions, i.e., it makes them follow a certain lawlikeness of rhythm and dynamism. But in setting such a lawlikeness discipline does not at all constrict and impede the body's activity. On the contrary, the rhythmic and dynamic orderliness of its motions expands the sphere of possibilities for such an activity, enables it to be truly free, and in this way brings it closer to *music*. It is for this reason that Plato, in the first phase of education, draws such a close connection between gymnastics and music. After all in ancient Greek music, too, rhythm and dynamics were much more important than melody or harmony. That's why it wasn't yet an independent branch of art. Most often it had an auxiliary function accompanying a declamation (recitative) or dance. To be sure, it seems it is the rhythm and dynamics of the music that determine the rhythm and dynamics of the dance, especially modern; and thus the latter has to adjust to the former. But if we look at the historical origin of choreography, the relation between dance and music will appear in a different light. For primitive peoples dancing is by no means just an entertainment; above all it is a special kind of religious ritual that consists of certain actions to which magical power is ascribed. A dance grows out of a certain stylization of these actions, i.e., bringing out their rhythm and strengthening their dynamics with an accompanying noise (or singing). Melody is as yet entirely lacking here or is limited to the repetition of two or three intervals. But what applies to the motions (actions) out of which a dance arises also applies to all bodily motions performing this or that function, including those on which sport is based. To the extent that it characterized by a certain regularity of rhythm and dynamics, sport also contains within itself special aesthetic possibilities that can be exploited and unfolded in one or another way, whereupon physical culture turns into aesthetic culture, one totally foreign to an artificial aestheticism because it grows out of its physical foundation and is based on whatever lies in the potentialities of the body and its activities. But this organic connection of physical education with aesthetic culture is of great importance to the former itself. By broadening the body's aesthetic possibilities, it not only fosters physical prowess but also shapes spiritual culture by taking root in the latter as an essential moment of its structure and thereby becoming physical (body) culture in the strict sense of that word. Therefore the aesthetic aspect of physical culture cannot be regarded as a subsidiary thing, and a teacher should never lose sight of that aspect. It is equally important to both girls and boys: exercising the sense of rhythm and dynamics trains their sensitivity not only to the purposiveness and harmony of their own bodily motions but to all the rhythmic and dynamic phenomena in the world around them as well; it is thus that *aesthetic taste* is enabled to mature. Or, to put it differently, a true culture of the body gives rise to the love of beauty. By the same token, the sphere of a student's spiritual life broadens and deepens; he acquires an ability to perceive and upon perceiving to internalize such values as would be inaccessible to him if he lacked sensitivity to rhythm and dynamics.

But the effect of aesthetic education reaches even further: by broadening an individual's possibilities of perception and enriching his inner world, it also greatly improves his *sense of personal well-being*. Usually the timidity and bashfulness of children comes from lacking confidence in their physical abilities, feeling that they're clumsy, awkward, and cannot do anything right with their bodies. Anyone who was bashful and fearful as a child knows how much he suffered if he didn't dare, or wasn't able, to take part in the games of his classmates or compete against them for first place. Often the consequences of these sufferings are inerasable; the psychical wounds they inflict do not heal, giving rise to an *inferiority complex*; and then that person increasingly succumbs to those depressing emotions (for example, resentment, too great a susceptibility to insult, suspiciousness, and so on) that arise from a wounded self-love and feelings of powerlessness, thereby poisoning his whole life. To avoid these negative consequences of bashfulness, it is first of all necessary to restore a child's feeling of self-confidence. Amd this can only be done with a kind of physical education that gives due weight to the aesthetic factor.

A human being's cultural life can be improved not only by removing the causes of suffering but also by opening up new vistas of joy and things to be appreciated. And one of the greatest well-springs of joy, at the very least in one's young days, is the human body and the aesthetic possibilities that are to be found in it.

PROTECTING THE CULTURE AND
THE BEAUTY OF THE PAST

In our times a new attitude towards the state has become predominant, one that differs fundamentally from the liberal political ideology of the 19th century. According to the latter the activities of the state are limited to the protection of citizens' freedoms and rights. Now the function of the state is taken to be much broader: it has to lead the entire cultural life of the nation, not only managing the social and economic relations of its citizens but also stimulating the growth of its spiritual culture and setting the general direction of its development. From this there arise many new tasks and responsibilities for the state: it must not only concern itself with present-day issues but also make allowance for the nation's future.

Now the future cannot be envisaged if at the same time no attention is paid to the past. Cultural life is an organic process which can proceed forward only to the extent that a nation is able to make use of those resources of material and spiritual energy that have been husbanded by its preceding generations; i.e., to the extent that it knows itself. But such a self-knowledge requires that a nation not only be concerned with the productions of the present but also have a cognizance of its past and an awareness of the meaning of its historical legacy. The remembrance and experience of the past is not dead ballast that should be gotten rid of as soon as possible. Both for a conscious individual and a conscious nation it is alive and fructifies their everyday life and activity.

This is especially true of the arts.[1] New styles very often arise under the influence of very much older ones (compare the significance of the art and poetry of antiquity to the evolution of art in Western Europe or the influence of the sculpture and ornamentation of primitive peoples on contemporary decorative art). Therefore, a state that is genuinely concerned about the flourishing and development of artistic culture and spiritual culture in general must devote special attention to the protection of art works. These constitute the treasury of a nation's culture the neglect of which would be an irreparable dereliction.[2] To this end museums are not enough because the monuments of the past housed in them have been lifted out of the environment for which they were intended and to which their creators had adapted them. That is why museums cannot give us a fully specific and revealing picture of artistic life in the past.[3] Still, *architectural creations* are in this respect in a more favorable position than other kinds of art works. They remain where they have been built. But for them their environment is especially important and essential.[4] It to some extent determines their individual features and variations of style. In a word, the edifice in its surroundings forms one organic and harmonious whole (ensemble). Therefore it is incumbent upon people not only to provide for architectural monuments the requisite protection and renovation but also to ensure that their environment not be allowed to deteriorate or change in ways that clash with their style or function. From this it is clear that the *landscape itself, the very beauty of the surrounding nature is an unconditional cultural value* that must be protected from unnecessary damage and vandalism. It awakens the creative powers of contemporary human beings in the same way that it stimulated and inspired the creativity of past masters (let us just recall the significance of the Lithuanian landscape for the paintings of Čiurlionis). Of course, the onslaught of civilization greatly changes the overall look of various countries. And these changes are unavoidable. Nevertheless, we should try to make sure that at least the most beautiful and historically significant localities in Lithuania stay untouched, since they make possible a rather vital contact with the past and with the historical life of the nation. Until now, unfortunately, this important historical task is almost totally denigrated by us. And aesthetic concerns are always forced to take a back seat to purely economic and self-serving interests. Needless to say, such an attitude toward aesthetic values is incompatible with the the main direction that the cultural politics of our time takes. Of course, broadcasting a new political ideology is much easier than implementing it in all fields of culture. However, if the Lithuanian government is serious about its cultural responsibilities it cannot ignore these pressing questions of aesthetic culture and must with all means at its disposal resist that utilitarian attitude toward art monuments and natural beauty that has taken hold of our society.

The government must take the initiative to establish a *cultural foundation*. And we hope that the cultured classes of Lithuania will support such an endeavor as much as possible.

Endnotes

1 For example, in order to clarify, discern, and understand the nature and elements of a "Lithuanian style," it is necessary not only to keep track of folk art narrowly understood, but also to collect and preserve art works of the past in general as well as to pay attention to various manifestations of past epochs of art in Lithuania. Only then will we be able to distinguish what we have in common with our neighbors and what is strictly our own, peculiarly Lithuanian.

2 In Lithuania too little is done to collect and safeguard the art of the past: in the absence of a law protecting cultural treasures, not even that which is the least transient in this respect, the monuments of architecture, is being properly protected. For example, even though there is a great deal of talk about Vytautas

the Great, almost no one is concerned with properly protecting the architectural monuments of this period. Almost all the Gothic buildings of which there aren't very many in Lithuania anyway have during the last twenty years either been damaged by badly done renovations or totally destroyed. Thus in spite of pleas and protests from the admittedly powerless former Archaeological Commission (there being no law on the protection of monuments and no legal sanctions against damaging them), the Gothic churches at Skaruliai and Zapyškis continued to suffer the inappropriate "repairs" of their owners. Instead of tiling the Skaruliai church received a corrugated iron roof totally at variance with the architecture's ancient character (and this even though there is a high and visible Gothic roof giving the whole building its character!). The Zapyškis church, already frequented by flooding, continues to be damaged by human hands as well. Recently somebody again removed its ancient organ with the moving wood sculptures (David playing the harp). The incessant renovations and "decorations" of the Vytautas Church in Kaunas, done not by architects under the guidance of historians, but by all kinds of amateurs and construction engineers, also seem not to bother anyone. The architctural problems of old edifices should be solved not superficially, by blindly imitating ancient forms, but by delving into them deeply and supported by a thorough historical knowledge of the past epochs involved. This task requires a good acquaintance with all those characteristic formal elements that are called "style" and are covered by the concept of "the spirit of the age." A historically oriented architect is a true scholar of his field. He needs a feeling for art, a trained taste, a certain level of artistic and general culture, and, above all, an immense devotion and conscientiousness in re-creating. But if that is lacking, it is better to follow the principle everywhere observed in Europe: *hands off antiquity!* The same must be said about St. George's church in Kaunas, a Gothic edifice from Vytautas's time, built in the early 15th c. Its exterior has suffered considerably from "repairs" and "renovations," not to mention devastation of its surroundings. Further away from the city many churches and chapels hailing from this period have had their arches broken, their sophisticated architectural decorations cut off, and so on. Even the Vytautas church in Kaunas several times faced this fate because certain "decorators" and "artists" were inconvenienced by the remains of ancient architecture.

3 This is not at all to say that we don't need museums. Of course we do—just as much as we need schools and libraries. They have to elevate a society's cultural level as well as to familiarize broad sections of the public with the past. In addition, museums are a valuable study source for scholars and artists.

4 Unfortunately, little attention is paid to this even in such a city as Kaunas (not to mention the provinces). Just one example is the continuous disfiguring of City Hall Square (the ecclesiastical "museum," the bishop's palace).

THE ISSUE OF NATIONAL CULTURE

The question of national culture is nowadays a pressing one nearly everywhere, especially in those countries that have become politically independent since the Great War and the Russian Revolution. Now nearly everyone recognizes the positive value and significance of nationality. Even the Social Democrats, who previously totally rejected this principle as a great impediment to the bringing together of, and championing solidarity between, all nations, increasingly subscribe to the view that nationality itself, insofar as it is properly understood, does not conflict with humanity and with the universality of human culture. On the contrary, humanity, being something general and abstract, can become embodied in life and manifest its significance and creative power only by accommodating itself to humanity's real nature and to the concrete circumstances of its historical existence; in other words, the quality of being human can asserts itself only by becoming individualized and specific. The *principle of concreteness that implements this process of individualization is nationality*. It gives to humanity a certain special and unique expression. And only impregnated by the attributes of nation, race, and other concrete factors does humanity really become a creative force capable of advancing the development and improvement of culture.

Having acknowledged the value of nationality and having resolved to foster a culture based on it, we must first of all become fully clear on what it means and how it can be validly and fruitfully applied. A lot is being written on nationality nowadays, maybe too much. But a review of the literature unfortunately leads us to the conclusion that most of it does not help us to understand this problem in a deeper and more accurate way. What then should be the road leading us to a deeper and more understanding of nationality? Perhaps the most important thing is to look at nationality concretely. Concreteness is that paramount requirement that every philosophy, every worldview must satisfy if it is to acquire practical significance and stimulate the progress of culture. Our age, characterized as it is by a strictly practice-oriented attitude, highly values concreteness because it senses, even if only instinctively, what danger lurks in the abstract sciences that aim to fix and improve life without regard to its concrete features and circumstances. Taken abstractly even the most valuable element can turn into a negative value. This is a fact that everyone seriously concerned with the thriving of nationality should take into account. The national principle, if separated from the concrete totality of life, inevitably degenerates into a factor negatively affecting the course of culture.

Let us explicate this general thought with a bit more detail.

First of all the question arises, Is the nationality of a living nation something complete in itself and strictly delineated so that one may accurately define it by indicating a certain totality of limited features and characteristics? If this were so, then nationality would depend only on the past and a national culture would only have to follow past examples. The function of the nationality principle would be purely conservative: to ensure that the treasury of cultural goods created and assembled in the past is preserved for the future. Now obviously the development of culture demands that what has been acquired in the way of art, knowledge, religion, and social life not disappear and be used in an appropriate way. Yet, on the other hand, it is absolutely clear that if the role of nationality in culture were limited to such a conserving function then in the sphere of culture there would be no true creativity. The present generation would have to content itself with safeguarding the way of life inherited from its forefathers and with recreating in all fields of culture the forms vouchsafed by tradition. Of course, few would defend this position expressed in such a stark way. Nevertheless it is accepted by all who are inclined to take folk art, for example, or the language of village folk as a norm that contemporary art and literature should follow. Folk art and folk language took shape in such surroundings and under such circumstances as, by and large, no longer exist. They reflect a way of life and an attitude towards the environment that belong to the past and gradually cease to exist because they no longer correspond to present needs and demands. Of course, this doesn't mean that all this folk creativity has lost its value. It remains priceless as material or, to be more precise, as potential that our contemporaries must acquire and make proper use of. But in no case should we regard it as a regulative norm. For then art and literature become artificially primitive, unable to create anything truly new and valuable. Or we succumb to fruitless romantic fantasizing, lose sight of life's real tasks, and idealize things that no longer have any vitality and are slated to die. What's more, it is only through the mediation of the present that the past itself becomes available to our understanding. Only when we flow with the rhythm of current life and grasp its special way of action do we gain the sensitivity that allows us to find in the past that which can revive itself and flower anew in current circumstances. But even the present insofar as it is actual points to the future, and the goals and aspirations (tendencies) of the here-and-now can be realized only in the future. Hence it is never rigidly and unequivocally determined (circumscribed) but contains within itself a great number of possibilities each of which can in its own way become reality. Which of these possibilities is the one that'll be realized depends on the will of the subject, the nation itself. From this it follows that not only the nation but also its being national (its national ownness) is something that is constantly becoming, changing, developing. And this process of becoming and developing is contingent not only on external circumstances, on the historical situation but most of all on the nation itself, on its spiritual energy and intellectual self-determination. It is the nation itself that shapes its way and style of life, that forms its own ideals; and by turning these ideals to reality, it fashions and creates its national culture. That's why it's very often impossible to foretell in advance which form or type of art, literature, or social system is attuned to the spirit of the national culture and which is not. A firm answer to this question must usually await the culture's further development; only then will we know whether a certain given cultural form or tendency can organically coalesce with the national culture as a whole and become an essential part of it.

But the overvaluation of the past, together with the romanticism to which it gives rise, is not the only threat to authentic national culture. The latter also faces an all-important question, What should its relation to other cultures be? This is a question especially pressing to nations whose culture is young and only beginning to asserts itself. Will it be able to defend and preserve its individuality when it makes contact with the mature and well-formed culture of older nations? Perhaps it would be better for a young nation, at least at the dawn of its culture, to separate itself from other nations and to restrict cultural interactions with them? But from what source then will its spiritual forces derive nourishment, from whence will it draw that inner energy which the process of cultural creativity demands? From the historical traditions of its past, from the everyday ways and lifestyle of its common people? But that would mean succumbing to the romanticist temptation in an even worse way: it would consign the national culture to getting stuck in a petty, fruitless *provincialism* that inevitably constricts the intellectual horizon, lowers the level of mental alertness, and allows one to be satisfied with, and even proud of, the humblest results. Now self-important provincialism goes hand in hand with lack of understanding of, and contempt for, other nations, resulting in *blind intolerance and narrow-minded chauvinism. In the process of a nation's cultural maturation, just as in the development of an individual, the most important moment is the emergence of self-consciousness and self-knowledge.* But one can attain self-knowledge only through communicating with, and getting to know, others. That is why a national culture cannot grow at all without the influence of other cultures. In becoming acquainted with the ways other nations live, create, and think and in adopting as one's own whatever it regards as valuable and significant in these other ways, a national culture becomes aware of its own peculiarities and abilities; it learns to judge correctly its own potencies and powers and how to use them properly.

The influence of a foreign culture, as long as it's not degenerate, is neither harmful nor dangerous. It turns into a threat only if it is taken over in a mechanical way and at the same time manifests itself as a purely external civilization. For to make an alien culture one's own is not to mimic it to the point of being enslaved by it but is in fact to command its sources and so to transform it that it actually becomes an inalienable factor of one's national spirit. In other words, whether a foreign cultural influence turns out to the benefit or to the detriment of one's own nation depends entirely on that nation itself and the efforts it expends on real cultural work. They who are afraid of the influence of a foreign culture do not trust their own strength and admit they are too weak to adapt it to the features of their own nature. In any case they are hardly in a position to create an original and truly worthwhile national culture that has universal significance. In studying the cultural evolution of various nations we observe much the same process virtually everywhere. Each distinctive new culture develops under the influence of another already matured culture. At the beginning the latter indeed dominates; but as the assimilation process goes on the young culture gradually gains strength and letting its own forces assert themselves it reworks and reforms what it has assimilated to such an extent that a novel and distinctive cultural style comes into being. Almost all of the most important Western European cultural epochs were impregnated by ancient Greek culture (for example, the Roman, medieval, Renaissance, French classicist, and neohumanist cultures). The same can be said of the work of individual artists or thinkers. For example, Alexander Pushkin was most profoundly influenced by French literature and language. His style harbors quite a few gallicisms. And a French *esprit* decidedly shows through the way he thinks and perceives. Yet in spite—or perhaps just because—of that he became the founder of Russian classical language and poetry. In order that it awaken, true originality more often than not needs the impetus of external forces. In struggling with, and subordinating, them it finds and becomes conscious of itself.

Finally, we should not forget one more important circumstance: although a culture is created by the nation itself, its growth and development is nonetheless an organic process, one that depends on a special regularity and rhythm of its own. Therefore it can be regulated and ordered only according to an antecedent plan and only insomuch as this does not contradict its inner structure. It is not possible to force it at will into this or that desired direction or to increase the speed of this process. Every attempt thoroughly to rationalize it is never successful and often leads to contrary results: a certain cultural superficiality and artificiality, a falsification of the national character. *That which we should first of all strive for is not that one's culture be national but that it be deep. A human being's and a nation's creative powers awaken and become strong only when they dig deeply into their cultural work. A deep culture is by the same token organic, and an organic culture cannot be anything but national.* And true nationality is compatible with neither formality nor with hypocrisy.

One artist in whose work the spirit and individuality of the Lithuanian nation manifests itself most clearly and flawlessly is no doubt Čiurlionis. His creative ideas and aspirations are, however, purely artistic in nature; and the ideas which he embodies in his works are characterized by a supranational universality. The profundity (integrity) of his nationality that impresses us so much arises out of the exceptional creative efforts that he put into expressing his ideas in the language of colors and lines. What is truly significant and important matures and flourishes in silence. For the sake of national culture it is much more important to make cultural work deeper and to raise (perfect) its standards rather than decorate it with exterior tokens of nationality. Who will be responsible if one day the nation sees in its newly created culture not an ideal image of itself but a distorted and twisted face?

NEW DIRECTIONS IN CONTEMPORARY EPISTEMOLOGY

I

A third of the 20th century having passed, it's perhaps already time to take a look back at the road that philosophy has traversed during that time. Compared to the year 1900, the problematics of philosophy has changed quite substantially. This is evident not only from the fact contemporary philosophy is again interested in issues that some thirty years ago had been pushed out of scholarly philosophy and held to be inaccessible to scientific knowledge (for example, the principal questions of metaphysics), but also from the fact that even those problems that were current at the beginning of the 20th century are nowadays discussed differently and have a different meaning. In this essay we will throw some light on this significant change in the philosophical discussion, briefly concentrating on those issues that relate to the essence and structure of philosophical knowledge.

We will start from the problem of method. At the beginning of this century this problem was of primary importance, particularly in German philosophy. Various currents and schools of neo-Kantianism, even though they differed in their interpretations of Kant, had the same goal: to elucidate the transcendental method of criticism and to apply it to those new areas of knowledge that arose as science progressed. All problems of philosophy were subordinated to the problem of method. This tendency was especially pronounced in the Marburg school, which defined theoretical philosophy ("transcendental logic") as pure thinking about methods. True, already in the first decade of the 20th century neo-Kantianism had to cede first place to the phenomenology created by Edmund Husserl, but even that, though different in many essential ways from Kantianism, is first of all oriented towards method. The phenomenological method claims to ground and lead true philosophical knowledge; its foundation is an ideal intuition that grasps the essence of being itself. This intuition is immediate and objective. It directly intuits the phenomena themselves (rather than their representative symbols and abstractions). But in taking up these phenomena (these experiences), it shows no interest whatsoever in what is empirical in them, in what depends on their facticity, but concerns itself only with what is apparent to pure consciousness, with what constitutes the essential structure of phenomena. In this way it is different from all empirical and positive sciences. These sciences are based on facts. But the facts they treat of are not separate sensory data but *phenomena* that make up a certain unity of diverse elements or parts and are characterized by a certain peculiar structure. Therefore phenomena can be grasped to the extent their structure is *perceived*. Every positive science presupposes perception of the phenomena it investigates but does not explain it, i.e., it does not reveal the structure of the perceived phenomena. That is the task of phenomenological analysis.

From this it is clear that philosophy is a foundation for other sciences with respect not only to their object but also their method. Investigating the fundamental elements of all being, philosophy thereby also determines the method that grounds and invests with significance the ways of empirical knowledge. Only in virtue of its phenomenological method philosophy has become pure ontology (science of being) in the strict sense and thereby acquired a truly scientific character. Thus, or so it seemed, phenomenology perfected that reformation of philosophy that was begun by Descartes and continued by Kant but was completed by neither; for it succeeded in eliminating from philosophy all metaphysical presuppositions and in disclosing that starting point of knowledge that would guarantee its total trustworthiness. Furthering and developing phenomenological analysis and applying it to all the principal branches of knowledge, philosophy seemed destined to attain to real accuracy, and having reached it to march further on the same straight path on which the exact sciences has embarked. Yet these hopes faded. However important and fruitful it was, phenomenology along the way bounced up against major difficulties, which were inherent in its very nature.

The most important requirement of phenomenology is its demand that the method of knowledge completely adapt itself to the object of knowledge. It is only by looking at and seeing—and listening to and hearing—the object that one can grasp its special essence. In other words, for cognition to occur, the act of consciousness (intention) directed onto the object must correspond to the object's nature. But that act is first of all determined by the general attitude of consciousness. Therefore, the possibility of grasping this or that object depends on that attitude. Without an appropriate attitude of consciousness (mindset) the object is simply inaccessible to cognition. Such a necessary connection between knowledge and a fitting mindset is manifest in the phenomenological method itself. Ideal intuition or grasping of essences presupposes an *object-related* mindset whenever the object stands before the subject as something separate and independent. But by no means all phenomena can be accessed by this contemplative attitude of consciousness (for example, all "experiences" or sensations in the strict sense cannot). To perceive and understand them phenomenology cannot content itself with direct perception, it must use data that depend on a different (nonobjective) mindset. Of course, this does not negate the importance of phenomenological intuition but just shows that in performing its methodical role phenomenology inevitably must go beyond the limits it had set itself at the beginning.

There are other considerations which show that the phenomenological method is not self-sufficient. On the one hand, ideal intuition is able to grasp the essence of phenomena only by lifting them out of their empirical surroundings and rejecting all those moments that are influenced by external factors. Thus phenomenology cannot do without a certain *abstraction*, a certain *isolation* of the phenomena it investigates. On the other hand, ideal intuition could not reach its goal if it didn't merge directly with the phenomena themselves, if it didn't embrace all their concreteness, i.e., all that in which the real essence and structure of phenomena assert themselves. Consequently, phenomenology must be especially careful that the abstraction and isolation of phenomena it uses does not destroy their concreteness. But for the execution of this task ideal intuition often does not suffice. There are many phenomena whose nature can be thoroughly understood only from their relations to other phenomena. Taken separately, a phenomenon is indistinct, opaque, as it were silent; it does not tell the investigator what is important and essential to it. This feature is above all characteristic of those phenomena that are *significant*, i.e., whose essence also depends on what they mean to a human being and what part they play in his life. An example of such a phenomenon is knowledge (cognition) itself. One cannot fully understand its essence without regard to its significance and role in human existence. In other words, phenomenological analysis in those cases cannot end with an intuition that is "stigmatic" (i.e., based on isolation); it must also be "conspective," i.e., embrace those relations which the phenomenon enjoys with its environment. But such a conspective perception does not at all coincide with pure direct intuition; it often proceeds by detour and collects a phenomenon's nature from the way it responds to its surroundings. Sometimes the phenomenon has to be outsmarted in order that it speak up and show what it is really like.

From what has been said we may draw the following conclusion. The extraordinary importance of the phenomenological method to philosophy cannot be doubted. Philosophy can no longer dispense with it. Only with its help is it able to fortify its systematic constructions with truly clear and well-confirmed concepts. Nevertheless, we must admit that the phenomenological method lacks that universality and self-sufficiency that adherents of classical phenomenology ascribe to it. To become really fruitful and significant, it must be supplemented by other, indirect methods of knowledge. What are these? No general answer to this question can be given. That depends on the problem under investigation, i.e., on the special features of the kind (sphere) of objects in question. From this it is clear that the problem of method does not have the central place phenomenology has assigned to it; therefore, we can understand why at the present time it has lost much of its importance.

II

But the inner evolution of phenomenology does not stop there. It not only pushed the problem of method back into second place, it made prominent several other problems, essentially changing them and illuminating them anew. Such a change in problematics affected the essence of phenomenology and had great impact on the manner and direction of phenomenological philosophizing. Classical phenomenology proceeds from the supposition that with the help of ideal intuition the essence of phenomena can be accurately highlighted and abstracted from its empirical environment. In epistemological terminology this means that there is a strict and fully determinate difference between knowledge of *a priori* (not only formal, but material) moments or elements and knowledge of *a posteriori* ones. This sets the task for phenomenology: it must explain this difference and describe the structure and contents of *a priori* knowledge. But it is just this supposition that raises major doubts.

First, there is no general criterion that would allow a strict and always unambiguous separation of *a priori* and *a posteriori* regions of knowledge. The evolution of philosophy and science especially suggests a contrary conclusion, namely, that in concrete cases the boundary between *a priori* and *a posteriori* spheres of knowledge is relative and mobile. Of course, such an unclarity and fluidity of boundary may be due to the empirical inadequacy and innacuracy of our knowledge. However, the reason for, or cause of, it might lie deeper and be more fundamental. We should not forget that ideal intuition, in grasping and fixing the phenomenon's essence, always sees it abstracted from one important factor—real time. Let the phenomenon take place in time, let temporality constitute its essential determination: its essence (its "idea") rises above time's sphere of action; the essence (of the phenomenon) is supertemporal and in this sense eternal and unchanging. The independence of essence from the empirical (empirical being) also harbors its independence from time. However, the question arises, What grounds and confirms this changelessness and supertemporality on the part of essence? It is hardly something self-evident; denying it does not land us in absurdity. Thus we may surmise that the unchanging nature (supertemporality) of essence is not absolute but relative: it depends on certain changeable conditions. Or, to put it more precisely, supertemporality can be ascribed to phenomenal essence only in a *logical* sense insofar as the latter is taken as an idea. But ontologically essence is subject to factors that are closely connected with temporality. This claim is something that a deeper analysis of the problem of knowledge leads to. In defining the essence of knowledge we cannot be content with a stigmatic view of it and ignore all those relations by which cognition is connected with life. Such a definition would at the very least be one-sided, incomprehensive. But, additionally, nothing assures us that it isn't erroroneous or inaccurate; for it can ascribe to knowledge itself something that depends on the properties of certain unnoticed factors that underlie it. Those phenomena on which the phenomenological analysis of knowledge is based belong to the sphere of *human* knowledge. But the knowledge of human beings does not constitute an independent, complete totality which would be self-sufficient. Its structure, main tendencies, and development are determined by the function it performs in human existence. Consequently, the vital, specific essence of knowledge can be grasped only upon taking into consideration the very nature of man. But the constancy and time-independence of man's nature is a myth that the science of our time does not allow us to believe in. Neither from the biological nor the sociological nor even the ethical point of view can we find in human nature an unchanging nucleus, i.e., a totality of constant features, that would unambiguously define its concrete essence. This is a decisively important consideration that forced philosophers to undertake a fundamental review of the current situation of philosophy in its entirety. Phenomenology, too, had to take account of it, with interesting consequences for the direction of its research. The older generation of phenomenologists (Edmund Husserl, Alexander Pfänder, and others) were interested mainly in analyzing the formal *a priori* elements of knowledge. The younger generation led by Max Scheler began to delve into the material side of the *a priori* sphere. That means that the focus of phenomenological thought moved away from more abstract problems to those more concrete and closer to reality itself. And this reality, taken concretely, is the human environment, the *Umwelt*, the world the human being not only knows, but also judges and affects; in a word, it is that in which his hold life is rooted and unfolds. That is why the problem of man arises anew as the main problem of contemporary philosophy, and *philosophical anthropology* becomes that area of research in which the most important thinkers of our time (Max Scheler, Martin Heidegger, Karl Jaspers) do their work.

III

Together with philosophical anthropology the problem of *facticity* (Faktizität) emerges as the most urgent theme in current philosophizing.[1] Facticity does not coincide with empirical experience or empirical investigations.

It is not the pure facts themselves nor the sum or collection of these facts. Facticity is just their essential terrain, to be apprehended only through the concrete connection of facts, the concrete unfolding of events in which a reflective human being finds himself; in other words, through his actual, essential situation, which determines his interaction with the surrounding world. Thus the perception of facticity is nothing other than an understanding of this actual situation, its *ontological interpretation*. Seeking to come closer to reality itself, to make direct contact with it, philosophy has to take cognizance of how reality concretely manifests itself in the human being. And this concrete manifestation of reality can be described by only two things: *facticity* and *actuality*. Of course, this doesn't mean that the question of facticity exhausts the entire problematics of philosophy. Even so it is one of its most important aspects, which philosophy had for a long time totally neglected and whose significance it has only now fully grasped.

With the emergence and stepping forward of this new aspect, a further change in philosophical problematics took place: the *problem of time* acquired a major importance not only for ontology, but the theory of knowledge as well. Looking more closely at the history of philosophy, we are struck by the fact that from the very beginning all its efforts were directed toward one goal: to shed temporality, to get out of the sphere which is under the power of time. In truth, as soon as philosophy appeared out of the mists of myth it raised the question, What is the original beginning of all things, that element from which all is born and to which all returns? The most essential feature of this element is that it is indestructible, constant, and unaffected by any alterations undergone by all other things. The more philosophy developed and deepened, the more exactly and clearly it tried to grasp and express in words the changelessness and supertemporality of this element. In Plato's theory of ideas this view received its most lucid and perfect expression. Real (pure) Being is the world of Ideas rising above the sphere of being and becoming; in its essence it is eternal and self-identical. On the other hand, the sphere of sensible phenomena, dependent on the regularities of time and becoming, is unreal and apparent being, i.e., being mixed together with nonbeing and thus condemned to wither and die. It is an imperfect image of ideas and receives being from its eternal prototype. Even in those theories that ascribe to the first element a certain mobility or dynamism, this mobility or dynamism is conceived as something static, something that does away with both temporality and the change that occurs in time. Even Hegel's system does not constitute a real exception here because the dialectical process by its essence is not temporally conditioned.

Yet it is not in philosophical speculation that this conception of the relation between being and time first emerged. Its most important impulse is inborn to the very structure of thinking and corresponds to the natural course and inner evolution of thought. Isn't all human knowledge based on concepts? But a concept, in answer to the question, What is an object?, brings out its "essence," that which is common to phenomena and things, which circumscribes their groups and kinds, in other words, that which does not depend on the individualizing features of "here" and "now," i.e., is not contingent on real time. Thus the problem of knowledge itself compels us to turn our eyes toward the atemporal sphere of concepts (ideas) and to look for the elements of being not just with the help of this sphere but directly in it. What's more, the same tendency is manifest in prescientific thought, in sensory perception itself. In the world picture that emerges in every human being's consciousness the fundamental structural element is a *thing*. And a thing is conceived by us as a certain bodily substance, the qualities and states of which can change but it itself remains the same as long as it exists. In addition, the image of the thing with regard to its structure depends on space rather than time. Hence the natural worldview of man gives primacy to those things that tend to be steady and are less influenced by time. The same path is taken by scientific knowledge, which endeavors to explain the material world as a completed system of certain constant elements, a system governed by unchanging and strictly defined laws.

It is the great merit of Henri Bergson that he was the first to call attention to and more accurately explain the fundamental significance of this tendency of thought and knowledge, which attempts as much as possible to banish time from our worldview or at the very least to pull it into a static scheme that can be juxtaposed to the structure of space and subordinated to supratemporal lawlikeness. It may be that the biological interpretation of this tendency is insufficient and even wrong; but the analysis of sensory perception and temporal and spatial relations begun by Bergson and later continued by other philosophers convincingly showed that the point at which philosophy starts is itself a problematic matter requiring examination and justification. It is not at all self-evident that being, ontologically speaking, is prior to becoming, or, in other words, that the first element(s) of being is (are) unchanging, eternal, supertemporal, and, conversely, the reality that depends on time, is secondary and dependent. The fact that our knowledge cannot dispense with general concepts not dependent on time and that it always attempts to base becoming on certain constant, atemporal elements, is not sufficient to justify or ground this conception of being; it itself is in need of explication.

This general doubt is confirmed by another significant circumstance: all systematic attempts hitherto undertaken to deduce becoming from elements independent of time have failed, and this failure is not accidental. Time and temporality are something special, incomparable, irreducible to other principles. Therefore, either all philosophical theories that accord priority to unchanging and supertemporal elements are incoherent (they surreptitiously, in one or another form, presuppose time), or they totally avoid the problem of time and fail to notice its crucial importance.

IV

Lastly, the dissemination of scientific experience and scientific theories demolished the factual foundation of this conception, i.e., all those presuppositions that seemingly corresponded to reality. In general, we can describe this direction of the evolution of knowledge as follows: the sphere of being held to be independent of time is getting narrower and gradually disappearing, while the spere of becoming and temporality is constantly expanding and slowly taking over all of the reality to which human beings have access.

This process first of all affected the sensible world and fundamentally changed its scientific understanding. Heraclitus' saying *panta rei* is fully acknowledged by the natural sciences of our time. The constancy and substantiality of things turned out to be just an illusion or, more precisely put, an aspect of physical phenomena that depends not so much on nature itself as on man's psychophysical organization and the structure of his perceptual acts. On closer look it became clear that things are nothing other than certain cutouts from the physical processes occuring in nature, certain complexes of active unity and material energy to which constancy and substantiality are ascribed only because their change, when compared to the rhythm of human organic existence, is much slower and cannot be directly observed.

But however much the scientific conception of the physical world differs from the naïve worldview, the former's fundamental view remains the same or at least the view of classical physics does, since it puts at the foundation of its construction certain constants, certain steady factors whose identity is wholly unaffected by becoming. These include, first of all, those ultimate elements out of which matter is constituted (atoms or electrons) and the amount of matter or energy, and secondly, such formal and structural factors as three-dimensional space and the laws of nature, i.e., all those specifications of causality that underlie the relations of material elements and their complexes in space and time.

To these constants we must add the so-called laws of logic, which enable the definition of all natural phenomena and their relations. To the extent that the objectivity of scientific knowledge is recognized, their objective significance cannot be doubted.

V

The radical break in the scientific worldview began with doubts about the constancy of the constants, i.e. when the belief in their changelessness was confronted by facts contradicting it. To be sure, not all of the constants mentioned are of the same type and significance. Some are purely formal and seemingly necessarily tied to the very structure of the phenomenal world; hence, the champions of transcendentalism ascribe to them the power of *a priori* principles. Other constants are nothing but presuppositions without which science is impossible but the necessity of which is neither self-evident nor can be demonstrated. Finally, there are constants derived from experience by the method of generalization. The constancy of these constants is not necessary. The further development of experience can show that their constancy is only relative or even just alleged. And concerning the general presuppositions or postulates on which science is based, their epistemological significance is still unclear and not fully determined. Perhaps they are successful predictions that have preempted empirical generalizations. But perhaps with the progress of science some of them might be reduced to *a priori* elementary propositions. In any case it is only the first sort of constants that are of fundamental importance to the structure and essence of knowledge. Their *a priori* necessity guarantees the supertemporality of the elementary principles of knowledge. If this necessity is denied, the firm foundation of knowledge collapses. It is precisely in this direction that the evolution of contemporary science progresses. That is why the current crisis in the foundations of mathematics and physics severely impacts on epistemology as well.

Let us give some examples. In his transcendental aesthetics Kant determined and grounded the *aprioricity* of space. The intuition of infinite, uniform, three-dimensional space is a necessary condition of the phenomenal world. This view was accepted by the majority of idealist philosophers; but even among mathematicians interested in the philosophical foundations of geometry it had quite a few adherents. Kant's thesis implied two propositions: (1) that another (non-Euclidian) structure of space can neither be thought about nor represented and (2) that within the confines of the phenomenal world Euclidian geometry represents the structure of real space. Today neither of these two propositions can be truly affirmed, at least in the sense that was given to them during Kant's time. First, a more thorough analysis of the foundations of geometry has shown that Euclid's geometry is by no means logically necessary and that on the basis of other axioms one can construct a number of consistent geometrical systems describing the nature of space entirely differently (for example, the geometries of Lobachevsky and Riemann). To be sure, this conditional nature of geometric axiomatics does not yet prove the falsity of Kant's thesis. If only a homogeneous three-dimensional space could be imagined (depicted) and if it corresponded to the structure of the sensible world, then Euclidean geometry would preserve its *a priori* validity. However, with the confirmation and acceptance of the theory of relativity, one must wholly renounce the formally *a priori* conception of geometry and recognize that real space is not something empty and without any physical properties, but a field of physical forces whose structure depends on the distribution of the energy disseminated in it and changes as the potential of forces changes. In that case space is inseparably connected to time, and geometry is not a self-sufficient formal science but closely connected to physics and its empirical development. In other words, geometry, as a science of real space, ceases to be a purely *a priori* discipline, while the constancy of its constants turns out to be relative and contingent on empirical factors. Of course, this doesn't mean that Euclid's geometry has lost its scientific value but only that it performs the function of an ideal system that can be applied to the human environment but that in no way corresponds to the real structure of the physical world.

Another example is provided by the evolution of the concepts of matter and mass. Matter is the opposite of empty space. These two concepts are correlative; this at least is how they appear to thought that bases itself on our everyday experience. A picturesque prototype of matter is a hard body (thing), not a liquid or gas. It has all the physical properties; its nature underlies those features through which the reality of matter is revealed to us: mass, gravity, resistance. Therefore hard bodies constitute, so to speak, the skeleton of our surrounding world. A human body is somewhat different, and it is primarily hard bodies that it can use as instruments with which it affects and changes its environment. Finally, hard bodies serve in cognitive tasks as well, both practical and theoretical; they fulfill the functions of measures and weights since, compared to liquids and gases, they are characterized by constancy of shape and size. Keeping in mind all these qualities of hard bodies, it is entirely natural to think that the elements of matter are nothing other than the smallest hard bodies (corpuscles). On this basis the other states of matter—fluidity, gaseousness and their changes—can be explained as resulting from a certain spatial distribution of matter. From antiquity up to our time the *atomistic* theory underwent a long and rather complicated evolution. For as long as matter was held to be a substantial element of the physical world and opposed to empty space, atoms retained the guise and features (weight, mass, resistance) of hard bodies.

But ever since the ascendancy of electromagnetic theory, which not only unified different branches of physics but also subordinated chemistry to physics, the hard body ceased to the prototype of matter.

The place of the atom as the simplest element of the physical world was taken over by the electron and the proton.[2] Now electrons and protons are not material particles or corpuscles in the true sense; even though they have mass assigned to them, this mass depends first of all on the electrical charge and its voltage. And if physics talks about electrons (and protons) as small balls with a diameter, this indicates only the smallest distance that is possible between the centers of two electrons. Thus, each electron or proton has to be regarded as a center of force or energy, independent of any material possessor of them. This shows that matter is not a primary element of the world, but a secondary, or derivative, phenomenon. Mass and gravity are essential characteristics not only of matter, but of every kind of energy. Hence an increase in a body's kinetic or thermal energy is accompanied by an increase in its mass. Thus the quantity of matter is not constant; matter can turn into one or another form of energy, and vice versa. That's why we may surmise that matter is nothing but a special kind of energy. But if so, if energy is the foundation of matter and not the other way around and if energy doesn't need a substantial (material) owner, then, it seems, the strict difference between space and matter vanishes and both members of the opposition get closer to each other. Particles of matter, being centers of energy, do not essentially differ from the force field surrounding them: they can be understood as special modifications of this field, as points where the tension of forces reaches an especially high degree and a certain static equilibrium comes about.

In connection with this new conception of space and matter and their relations, there emerged in physics a most significant tendency: to harmonize and unite into a systematic unity two opposed theories of physical energy that hitherto had been thought as excluding one another, i.e., J. C. Maxwell's electromagnetic wave theory and the corpuscular theory. The first holds kinetic energy to be vibrations of waves of aether, thus ascribing energy to the field of action itself. Therefore the undulation of the aether is a continuous process not only in the sense that it is continuously diffused in space but also in the sense that all its changes (in velocity and intensity) are continuous and pass through all intermediate phases between the initial and the final degree. According to the corpuscular theory, on the contrary, energy can be released and absorbed only in discrete quantities that are all multiples of the smallest, the quantum. Thus the quantum in this theory plays the part of the atom, so a rise or fall in the energy level takes place in jumps. The most thorough examination of the data and the experimental checking of both theories showed that physics cannot dispense with either and that both have to be somehow merged in a systematic unity. This problem is being addressed by the newest theories of de Broglie, Schrödinger, Heisenberg, and Dirac. To that end they introduced into physics the new concept of *matter waves*, which may be explained as follows: every point of matter (the smallest material element) is not just a simple point taking up only one precisely defined place, it is also a packet of waves spreading out in a smaller or larger sphere. In indicating the location of a point of matter, the physicist can only be certain that it is located within this sphere but precisely where that is at any given moment can only be indicated with a greater or lesser probability. There's no need for us to delve further into the most important ideas of that theory, for physicists themselves have not yet agreed on how it should be formulated precisely and systematically expounded. Be that as it may, the general orientation of their thinking comes undoubtedly to this: matter and space, having previously been constants with a well-defined substantial structure, are turning into variables that can be determined only approximately within the limits of a system. A material point, accompanied by or even identified with a wave packet, has almost nothing in common with the image of a hard body that we are used to. Similarly, the dispersal sphere of matter waves is not identical to Euclidian space, since the undulations of these waves takes place in a so-called configurational space, the number of whose dimensions is greater than three and changes according to the quantity of degrees of freedom.

VI

But it may be objected to all these considerations that they fail to distinguish and even mix together the epistemological and the metaphysical side of the problem. The only thing that can be concluded with respect to the reformation of the main ideas of physics is that the principles which have previously been held to be constants turn out to be variable and thus have to be replaced by other, true constants justified by reality itself. In other words, this process of reformation describes only the evolution of natural sciences but not the structure of being (reality) itself, therefore it is not at all incompatible with the idea that the foundation of the real world consists of certain unchanging principles. Moreover, we must even admit or at least guess that such constants are an essential characteristic of nature because science in general cannot dispense with constants and all of its determinations (findings) have their ground in one or another system of constants.

But this objection leaves out of account that extraordinary direction in which the reforming of physical ideas takes place. It is not exhausted by the fact that one constant is replaced by another but is additionally marked by two more significant features: (1) the number of constants (enduring principles) gets progressivelly smaller and (2) they increasingly lose their *a priori* necessity and definition and turn into either simple empirical quantities whose stability is relative or ideal schemes that only approximately correspond to reality and do not describe its real, objective structure. That is what is shown by the examples mentioned. If space, according to Einstein's theory, in some ways resembles a mollusk whose structure and extension varies, then it is probable that these changes affect the dimension of space also, i.e., that the number of dimensions depends on what physical processes are actually going on in space. Absolute changelesness is attributed by relativity theory only to a purely formal moment, namely, to that mathematical regularity that describes the mutual relationships among different coordinate systems and thus allows the researcher to choose a system of coordinates at his discretion and move from one to another while the results of research do not change; this regularity also guarantees the invariance of natural laws and independence from the chosen point of observation.

The place of matter, which has lost the significance of a permanent substance, has been taken by energy. But the changelessness of energy ends with its *quantity*. Even though the principle of the conservation of energy does constitute the foundation stone of the natural sciences, it plays the part only of a necessary postulate; and it may turn out that it is valid for reality only approximately.[3] Therefore, if there is progress in the natural sciences, if the physics of our time has more deeply delved into nature and more closely approached to reality itself than the theories of former epochs, then it must be admitted that the traditional conception which has the natural order as something unchanging and which is based on a certain system of absolute constants has ever decreasing factual justification.

Only one kind of real constants, it appears, provides an exception: the natural laws that describe the relations of physical phenomena with respect to their quality and quantity. They are all variations and specifications of the causality principle, and their accuracy and strictness follows from the iron necessity by which this principle is characterized. It is the common foundation of all the exact natural sciences: they are valid only to the extent the principle of causality is objective. Of course, from Hume onward empiricist philosophy has doubted its real neessity and universality. But the natural sciences themselves never ceased relying on its objective significance and employed it as a universal *a priori* principle.

However, now it cannot be doubted that even this fortress of the traditional scientific worldview is crumbling. In truth, from that time onward when it was determined that the atom is not a simple element of matter, but is a system of electrons and protons, the physical and chemical properties of which depend on its internal structure and the electromagnetic processes taking place within it, atomic physics (microphysics) became the foundation of all macrophysics (molar physics). Now microphysics differs from macrophysics not only quantitively. Delving into intra-atomic phenomena made it clear that the principle of causality in the sense given to it by classical physics does not hold for them. This means that within the limits of quantum mechanics, to which intra-atomic processes belong, the laws of nature do not allow us unambiguously to fix the activity of any phenomenon (for example, the condition and velocity of a moving electron at any time); all the determinations reached by the investigator remain only approximate, i.e., end in a greater or lesser probability whose value is governed by the law of high numbers. To put it differently, in microphysics the laws of nature cease to be accurate and turn into statistical laws. How is such an indeterminacy of microphysical phenomena to be understood? Does it depend on the nature of the observer and the conditions of observation (the experiment), i.e, the imperfection of the instruments used, the inaccuracy of human senses, or the limitations of man which prevent him from comprehensively evaluating all the factors impinging on the phenomenon under investigation and accurately measuring their degree of influence? If the indeterminacy lay in subjective factors, an ideal observer would be capable of removing it and the probability's upper limit would approach one. But in fact, as experiments show, this limit is less than one. Consequently, the reason for this indeterminacy lies in the nature of the microphysical phenomena themselves, i.e., in a feature of theirs that is incompatible with the the strict validity of the causality principle. What are the general conditions on which the objective meaning of causality depends? (1) Determining that two phenomena, A and B, are connected by the causal tie, i.e., that A unambiguously causes B and that if A occurs then B, too, invariably occurs, is possible only in case both these phenomena can be somewhat isolated. Such a possibility of isolation is objectively grounded in the fact that the process investigated is somewhat independent and is not determined by other concurrently occurring processes. (2) Where isolation is possible, repeatability of the same (or similar) conditions is possible too; this repeatability allows an inductive generalization; in other words, the occurrence of the process (the connection of phenomena) does not depend on real (world) time. Therefore all natural laws determined by classical physics (except the second principle of thermodynamics) do not take into account real time and are equally valid for each moment of time.

But in investigating microphysical phenomena these conditions on the objective validity of causality cannot be fulfilled, and here's why. (1) Real time cannot be turned around. All physical processes take place in a certain direction defined by the Second Law of Thermodynamics. The life of the world as a totality is not cyclical, but historical, therefore no specific state of the world can repeat itself absolutely. (2) In addition, because all things in the world are related, there are not and cannot be processes that are totally independent and unaffected by surrounding (lateral) conditions. The phenomena investigated by macrophysics can be isolated only in such a way that all the factors that have but a minor impact on the process under investigation are simply ignored. Besides, the isolation is facilitated by the qualitative variety of the sensible phenomena which allows the researcher clearly to distinguish one kind from the other. In microphysics, by contrast, where we have to do with elementary processes, there neither is such a qualitative variety of phenomena—atomic and intraatomic processes end with the motion of electrons, the undulation of electromagnetic and matter waves—nor are there any such circumstances whose influence could be ignored. Consequently, if we wish to describe the activity of microphysical phenomena, we must take account of all the active factors without exception, including that influence which a certain phenomenon undergoes in virtue of the circumstances surrounding the experiment itself. But where one cannot isolate, there one cannot abstract from real time and from the actual state of the world dependent on that time; therefore, there can be no talk of a separate, somewhat independent process that would be unambiguously defined with respect to space and other aspects belonging to it.[4]

What conclusion follows from what has been said about the peculiarity of microphysics? Isolating the phenomena he is investigating and ignoring real time, the natural scientist, by using a method of special abstraction, fixes an ideal level in which he analyzes the connection and dependency of phenomena. It is only with respect to this level that he can reach accurate and unambiguous results. But this methodology cannot be applied to microphysical phenomena in the same way it can be to macrophysical ones. On the other hand, physics cannot do without the method of isolation for it alone guarantees the determinateness of the causal nexus. Hence in microphysics the ideal level of research has to be ascertained in another way, one corresponding to the nature of atomic and intraatomic processes: here the investigator takes note not of an individual elementary process, but of a certain group or class, as numerous as possible, of them, and statistically determines the general tendency dominant in that group. Consequently, this tendency characterizes the real course taking place in a totality of investigated phenomena, but with respect to an individual process it is ideal because it determines just its degree of possibility, its greater or lesser probability.

Thus we see that we cannot regard causality as a an (in the strict sense) objective principle independent of time, a principle governing the phenomena of nature and strictly determining their course. It is nothing other than an ideal schema, only approximately corresponding to reality and therefore not defining it unambiguously. But this approximate nature of the causal tie is due precisely to its not taking account of real time, i.e., of that condition that would guarantee the status of constants to the specific manifestations of causality, the laws of nature.

VII

There remains one more kind, the most important one, of constants, which is at the foundation of all the others. These are the so-called *laws of logic* on which the definiteness of all knowledge depends. But objective significance can be ascribed to knowledge only in case its determinateness reflects the determinateness of being itself. Thus the question arises, Do the laws of logic really play the part of ontological constants?

A more thorough analysis of various kinds of real being emphatically shows that not one of them exactly meets the demands of logical non-ambiguity and determinateness.[5] In fact, if we first of all review the thinglike objectual sphere of being dependent on the subject—our perceptions, sensory images, dreams—then in all these phenomena there anyway appears a greater or lesser unclarity, unvividness or ambiguity, i.e., one or another variety of a sensible logical vagueness. Of course, this vagueness is relative and manifests itself only within the limits of certain determinations,[6] but it constitutes a mark of the phenomenon which in a special way characterizes its sensory appearance. A similar vagueness, especially with respect to location and shape, is characteristic of all sensible non-thinglike, nonobjectual phenomena (for example, varieties of light and shade, aural impressions, and so on). The relation of logical principles to physical being that is independent of the subject appears somewhat different. But even here we do not find total or perfect correspondence. Real being, as we know, is not the world of constant things, but an incessant becoming and changing under the rule of time. But that which becomes and changes is, at very moment of becoming and changing, something incomplete, not yet fully determined, but in which there lies a multiplicity of different possibilities; something that the ancient Greeks called *apeiron*. In this regard becoming (changing) lacks univocal definiteness. To be sure, this doesn't mean that logical principles are altogether invalid for it. The undefinedness of becoming is not static, but dynamic. Of all the possibilities present with respect to every actual situation there happens only one, i.e., a certain well-defined possibility becomes actual. Consequently the process of happening is at the same time the process of determining (limiting) oneself. Only when it is over, i.e., no longer actual and turned into the past, does becoming acquire a univocal determinateness. Otherwise put, becoming meets the requirements of the logical principles insofar as these are taken not statically, but dynamically, i.e., not as conditions of complete determinateness but as the elements that govern the process of the self-determining (self-limiting) of becoming. This dynamical aspect of logical principles does not fit into the framework of pure rationality. It subordinates their validity to real time, since that which is still determining itself is not yet unambiguously determined and can, within the confines of temporality, never attain perfect determinateness.

Finally, the sphere of subjective or really mental being lacks the kind of determinateness that would correspond to logical principles. In its essence the mental world (our *I* and all its experiences, acts, and states) belongs to the non-thinglike, nonobjectual sphere of being. But logical determinateness is indissolubly linked to thinglikeness, objectualness. Hence the relation of mental being to logical elements can manifest itself only to the extent that the former in one way or another objectifies itself in thinglike phenomena, i.e., in bodily movements and actions, conscious images, or products of the "objective" spirit (language, myths, religion, art, and so on). But the objectifying process having been completed, its results reveal the same indeterminateness (ambiguity) that is characteristic of real becoming in the objectual sphere. Moreover, it must be pointed out that there is no total (perfect) correspondence between mental being and its objectual manifestations; i.e., our experiences do not unambiguously determine their specific ways of objectifying themselves. Therefore they may be interpreted in different ways. In this respect the irrationality of the mental world is still greater.

VIII

The general conclusions following from the scientific analysis of experiential data are already evident from what has been said above: in real being we do not find such principles, forms, or constants that would be (1) unchanging in a strict sense, i.e., totally independent of time, and (2) exactly (non-ambiguously) defined and completed (perfect). Or, in other words, there is no such changeless, supertemporal being that would be the foundation for becoming. In fact, in the process of becoming (i.e., the reality accessible to our experience) there manifest themselves only certain to some extent defined and constant tendencies. Therefore, that changelessness and determinateness that we see in both the internal and the external world is only approximately fixed and approximately accurate. When to such a tendency there is ascribed a perfect determinateness and an absolute (*a priori*) constancy, it becomes an ideal schema that only approximates reality and that cognition can use only insofar as it proceeds by abstraction and insofar as it analyzes reality on an ideal level created by abstraction. But knowledge in the strict sense, and especially scientific and philosophical knowledge, cannot do without abstraction, which is the most essential factor of its structure. Knowledge is born only at that moment when in the subject's mind there arises a judgment, i.e., an act that determines the object with general concepts. And general concepts constitute the ideal sphere of being. It follows that reality can be known only through the mediation of ideal reality.

This is a mysterious fact in need of explanation: Why can scientific cognition reach its goal only by going roundabout? Why does it manage to grasp and perceive the surrounding world only by reflectively creating abstract concepts and getting immersed into the sphere of ideal reality? Abstraction and reflection allow cognition to rise above the momentary concerns and interests of life, to gain some respite from the rule of real time, and to look from above not only at the surrounding world but also at the course of the subject's own life. Thus abstraction and reflection give knowledge a certain independence, thereby making it autonomous; but it gains this autonomy only insofar as it goes beyond the bounds of direct reality and takes root in the world of ideal logical being. In this way there appears a paradox in the course of scientific and philosophical cognition: *this cognition is able to perceive reality only by distancing itself from it.* This is a property that characterizes scientific (philosophical) knowledge but does not necessarily mark every kind of knowledge. Instinctive knowledge, which rules in the animal world and manifests itself, especially with the higher animals, in exceedingly well-developed forms performs its biological function without any reliance on abstraction and reflection. It always remains immersed in the environment of real existence, it reacts only to the stimuli of the actual moment, and still it excellently serves the organism's interests using the experience of the past and foreseeing the requirements of the future. If this is so, if cognition is not necessarily tied to abstraction and reflection, then these operations of thought are exceptional features of theoretic knowledge. Since theoretic cognition is characteristic of humans, then such a property of this type of cognition has to be in one way or another connected with human nature and its peculiar situation in the world. But before we delve into this question let us see how the above-described conclusions reached by 20th-century science and epistemology should affect the formulation and further treatment of the problem of knowledge.

From antiquity until our own times two opposed viewpoints fight it out in epistemology. According to one, knowledge grasps the real object itself and therefore it is the nature of this object that determines the structure of knowledge. This is the conception of *intuitive* knowledge; it recognizes the subject (mind) as a reality independent of the object known. Knowledge is essentially a passive act; it doesn't change anything in the data of experience. The second position, by contrast, holds the process of knowledge (cognition) to be *constructive*. It constitutes or creates the object known out of subjective impressions and experiences either by way of associations according to habits of thinking (as empiricism claims), or by way of the *a priori* forms of reason, the categories (Kant's transcendentalism). This idealist conception predominated in Western European philosophy, especially in the second half of the 19th century. Without a doubt it is an important achievement of Henri Bergson, other intuitivists (e.g., Nikolai Lossky), and especially of the phenomenological school that they revived the realistic conception of knowledge and defended its logical and factual basis. Knowledge wouldn't be what it means and couldn't be distinguished from other acts of the mind (for example, the imagination), if it didn't apprehend what really is or becomes, if it didn't present to the subject what is really there. Knowledge cannot be understood any other way, since without such an understanding of it knowledge ceases to be knowledge. That's why even idealism, although it looks at knowledge as a creative process, cannot in the end dispense with the conception of intuitive knowledge. In one way or another, it presupposes it even if it denies it in its ultimate conclusions. Besides, the analysis of the cognitive phenomenon itself shows unmistakably that knowledge starts not from the simplest elements but from the object as an intuition of a certain totality (unity of varieties) and that the process of synthesis and integration can take place only when a certain process of analysis and differentiation has already occurred. But having acknowledged the truth of the intuitivist position in principle, we must note that no intuitivist realist theory can make do with a conception of intuitive knowledge alone. Intuition, of course, remains the foundation of every cognition, but if it remained just what it is when taken by itself then scientific knowledge led by a search for truth could not emerge. Only upon differentiating itself does intuition reveal its content and acquire a logical form and significance. And giving an intuition logical form means translating it into the language of abstract concepts and objectifying it in the sphere of ideal being. Thus it cannot be denied that in cognition there asserts itself a certain activity of the subject. The subject not only apprehends the object, not only represents and recreates it in his consciousness, but also creates something novel. But what he creates is not the real object itself, but the concepts determining it and the logical relations of these concepts, i.e., that world of ideal schemas and ideas through which and in which knowledge becomes a special, self-sufficient arena of being and acquires a systematic structure. In addition, we must bear in mind that the formation of the intuition begins not with its logical differentiation but underlies its initial structure: intuition affords the subject only a certain aspect of the object that encompasses only a limited selection of its determinations and in which not all moments are equally important.

In other words, the structure and contents of this aspect depend on the subject's organic nature and the qualities of the the subject's environment. It would seem that this constructive nature of cognition could be used by idealism as an argument for its own position. But the idealist interpretation of knowledge does not take into account the organic connection of all logical constructions to the initial intuition itself. These constructions do not depend on a subjective attitude but grow out of the intuition's inner flowering and bear fruit only insofar as they bring to light those moments that potentially lie in the content of the intuition.

If we wish properly to understand cognition as an act though which the subject relates to his real environment, it is, in our opinion, important to emphasize that cognition is not just a contemplative act but an *activity* in the strict sense of the word. Usually epistemology analyses the cognitive act as something isolated whose relations to other acts is external and has no significance for its inner structure; whereas, in fact, the very first form of cognition, instinctive knowledge, has just an auxiliary function and is completely subordinated to the purposive activity which it must call forth. The transition to action is essential to such cognition and conditions its nature. Human knowledge, proceeding by abstraction and reflection, ceases to be dependent on external action, and having attained independence became contemplative in nature. Nevertheless its connection with activity did not vanish. The difference is only that activity has now become part of cognition itself and has to serve its own goals rather than just external (biological) ones. In a word, the activity with which cognition ends is nothing other than that logical formation and objectification of it that arises out of the primary intuition. In this respect cognition does not differ from any other real action: it changes something in the world; of course, not the object toward which it is directed, but the subject's relation to this object. At the same time there occurs a certain change in the ideal sphere in which the cognition objectifies itself. But ideal being, with the mediation of real subjects, enters into relations with real being and in this way itself acquires real significance and power. By creating ideal schemata and unfolding a system of concepts, knowledge thereby expands the sphere of being and allows the realization of hitherto non-existent possibilities. This is how the exceptional creative power of reflection and abstraction, those two principal features of objectual (objectifying) consciousness, manifests itself. But now matter how much reason rises above instinct and surpasses it in its possibilities, this difference is nevertheless based on the inner unity of both abilities. Idealism errs precisely in that it positions reason against nature as something entirely distinct and different. Conscious knowledge arises out of instinctive cognition; therefore, the ideal schemes created by reason, even if they do not fully correspond to real nature, nonetheless reflect its main tendencies and structural attributes. Hence, reason is able to subordinate nature (the phenomenal world) to its laws only because it itself is a creature of organic nature and never loses a vital connection with it.

But we must look at the possible conequences of the conception of knowledge we've just elaborated from another side. If knowledge is by its essence not just a contemplative but also a constructive act then this gives rise to a further complication of the problem of knowledge. Indeed, in the process of cognition there occurs in ideal being a certain change that somehow affects the real sphere, too. Consequently, the task of knowledge to apprehend reality as it really is, is burdened not only by the fact that real becoming and the dynamic processes of nature must be introduced into static scemata but also by the fact that the cognitive act itself alters reality to some extent. To be sure, this change does not affect the direct object of the cognitive act. But since an individual cognitive act constitutes only a certain element in a system of knowledge that must embrace the entire world, both the real and the ideal, then in the final analysis it cannot be denied that knowledge, even if only in an indirect way, does change (affect) its object. Therefore, when knowledge apprehends its object, we must also take into consideration its influence on the being that is known. This is a circumstance that traditional epistemology takes no account of. Or, more precisely, it doesn't recognize this fact in that it claims that theoretical knowledge is distinguished by pure contemplativity that does not really touch the object known. Contemplativity is undoubtedly the most essential mark of theoretical knowledge. Nevertheless, when analyzing knowledge concretely, i.e., with regard to its concrete manifestations in concrete surroundings, we must recognize that its contemplativity is relative and hence compatible (in the above-mentioned sense) with a certain constructivity. That pure contemplativeness on which classical epistemology is based is upon closer look nothing but an ideal postulate (ideal schema) that only approximately corresponds to reality and that somewhat stylizes it in the same way that the traditional view does that holds becoming (temporal being) to have a foundation in supratemporal, changeless being. It may even be said that these two theses claiming to describe the traditional view on knowledge are correlative. Pure contemplativity is possible only where the elements of being are constant and not contingent on time. On the other hand, changeless supratemporal being is accessible only to purely contemplative knowledge. The constructive moment in the act of knowledge affects its result, the knowledge obtained, giving it a certain indeterminacy (lack of univocal definiteness). In reality a completed and exactly defined system of knowledge would be possible only if being (the world) depended on a finite number of changeless, supratemporal elements, i.e., if being were essentially static. But reality is a process, a becoming.

And becoming cannot be derived from a system of unchanging principles; it seems not even to be dependent on exactly defined and constant laws. This relative indeterminacy of becoming is necessarily reflected in knowledge. Moreover, into real becoming there also enters a certain creative moment—at the very least to the extent it participates in, and is affected, by knowledge and the world of ideas (ideal schema) knowledge creates. This increases the indeterminacy of the course of becoming even more and at the same time lessens the univocity of knowledge and its evolution. Yet this state of affairs by no means forces the drawing of skeptical conclusions. After all, the newest physics, according to which the laws of nature are but statistical laws describing the general dominant tendencies in ongoing physical phenomena, does not succumb to skepticism but, on the contrary, manages to define concrete, real becoming even more exacly than does classical physics. We should not forget that the indeterminacy which lies at the bottom of knowledge itself is not absolute but relative, i.e., it asserts itself within the limits of a certain determinacy, and all new possibilities arise from the depths of a certain determinate situation. The creative or constructive moment in knowledge is far from coinciding with a blind accidentality.

IX

The consequences that follow from the review and revision of the problem of knowledge, however, do not stop with a change in the conception of knowledge itself but spread into the foundation of ontological knowledge, too. It cannot be otherwise. Determining a peculiar relation of the subject to the object, cognition (knowing) itself is a certain event in being (reality). That's why every epistemological view already is a certain interpretation of being. Realism and idealism, being opposite epistemological thought currents, solve the problem of being in different ways, too. But an analysis of the traditional forms of both currents shows that their ontological presuppositions also have something in common. This is evident from the fact that a perfect (scientifically worthy) knowledge must be univocally determinate. But knowledge can meet this requirement only when its object is a completed and thoroughly determinate thing. Now that which is completed and exactly determined is not contingent on real time; thus it is static and unchangeable, or at the very least, the principles that govern its changes rise above the sphere of time. It seems at first glance that a complete determinacy of this kind must be ascribed not only to knowledge but also to real being itself, for otherwise one could not distinguish one real thing from another. But such a characterization of being, as is clear from our analysis, does not correspond to the real state of things. Real being is process, and process lacks exact (perfect) determinateness. And if the object of knowing seems to us to be exactly defined (univocally determined), this depends not on the structure of being itself but on that *contemplative mindset* (attitude of contemplative consciousness) that is the foundation of theoretical knowledge. This mindset is based on a two-fold abstraction. First, it isolates its object by ignoring real time and the concrete situation that depends on time; second, it also abstracts itself from the concrete subject (observer) and his real relation to the object. Therefore, it is said that the subject, submitting himself to pure contemplation, is utterly passive and does not affect the object. Only an isolated object, i.e., one transferred onto the ideal plane by abstraction, acquires perfect definiteness. Usually the significance to knowledge of abstraction is not appreciated sufficiently. It not only governs the sphere of theoretic knowledge but also determines the structure of sensory perceptions. In fact the substantial elements of the sensory world are things (hard bodies), and all processes and changes taking place in physical being in one or another way depend on them. And the image of a thing is by its essence static and independent; it is not dependent on either time or the knowing subject. This is also true of abstract (scientific) knowledge: those concepts that are its structural elements are static, supratemporal unities. Thus we see that isolation, this inseparable moment of theoretic viewing (theoretic contemplation) creates a special way of seeing and perceiving familiar being, a way that can be described as *making thingly* or *objectifying*. This means that being on which contemplative consciousness focuses becomes an *object, thingly*; i.e., it acquires the nature of a static, self-sufficient, non-time-dependent item. But such a description of theoretic contemplation does not yet suffice: we must add that its prototype and sensory foundation is *vision*. The knowledge of the external world consists of data from vision and touch (in a broad sense). All other senses perform only an auxiliary function in joining up with visual and kinaesthetic impressions. But only vision determines that relation and that distance which pure contemplation requires in order for the phenomenon perceived to acquire the independence and static unity of an object. This is confirmed by the very language used in this connection: it is no accident that almost all these words derive from the sphere of vision (*theoria, idea, eidos, contemplation*, and others). If so, then only those moments that are founded on the data of vision can enter into knowledge justified by theoretic contemplation. Consequently, pure contemplation to some extent limits the sphere of phenomena accessible to scientific knowledge.

On the other hand, science cannot stop at a world conception reached by abstraction. Its goal is concrete reality itself. And the closer it gets to its goal the more it dispenses with all abstractions, which in the process of knowledge play only a scaffolding role. Therefore, science also has to rid itself of those abstractions that derive from the initial contemplative mindset. And actually we do see that in the world conception created by contemporary physics thingly independent substances have entirely given way to lawlike relations among phenomena. The static aspect has been replaced by a dynamical one; the dependence not only of real being but also of its lawlikeness on time was everywhere recognized. Concurrently the attitude toward the relationship of elements to their totality was changing. Previously it was thought that the elements are somewhat independent of, and ontologically prior to, to the totality that embraces them, whereas now a contrary view has gained ascendancy: namely, that it's not the elements (the elementary processes) that sustain the totality (group, system), but it's the totality that as it were measures the elements and it's only the relationship of the elements to the totality that sustains their real significance and being. But all of these changes are not yet sufficient to overcome the abstraction inherent in the contemplative theory of physical being. One abstract moment still remains, namely, the dependence of this theory on the visible aspect of being. Although the physical world investigated by theoretical physics is not directly assessible to the senses, knowledge about it is based on data from vision and on the contemplative mental attitude that is peculiar to vision. But there are other attitudes of the subject in which he asserts his activity by affecting his environment and resisting its response. Here the distance between subject and object that vision needs vanishes, and the subject enters into contact with his surroundings directly with his body. Only such a touching and such an interaction with the external world allows the subject to experience and to feel the tension of forces and the actualization of energy. These sensations (experiences) are unavailable to pure contemplation. That's why the conception of the world that is based only on contemplation is inevitably one-sided and imperfect as it takes no account of data that go beyond the horizon of pure contemplation. For physics as a special science the world's contemplative aspect is the one best suited to desribe the world's material phenomena mathematically.[7] But this is insufficient for a philosophical worldview. Because it seeks to describe the essence of real being, it cannot ignore those of its features that arise from a human being's interaction with the external environment. From this it is clear that the issue of realism (what is real being?) arises anew and can be satisfactorily solved only on the basis of that new philosophical anthropology that regards the human being as a concrete totality and treats equally both man's contemplativeness and his activeness.

The physics of today compels realism finally to abjure the objectification of being. On the other hand, idealism, too, taking account of the consequences of contemporary biological and psychological research has to modify its view substantially. Reason (mind) and consciousness are not the independent and universal elements that rationalism and Kant's transcendental idealism thought they were. The conscious mind is rooted in instinctual reason and, to tell the truth, it just disseminates, differentiates, and objectifies that which is potentially in the latter. But instinctual reason, in its turn, is tied to the life and functioning of the body. Thus the activity of the mind depends on that of the body (organism). But if so, then those motives for idealism that have an objective foundation can be explained only by the same philosophical anthropology to which the problem of realism leads us. Therefore, a correct understanding of the opposition between idealism and realism is possible only within the framework of philosophical anthropology.

Finally, the question we raised above, Why does cognition acquire scientific significance only upon the creation of a sphere of ideal being and objectifying itself in it? can be adequately answered only by an anthropology that delves into man's specific nature. We will not pursue this question in detail but just point out two important considerations.

If the object of knowledge is the world which has given rise to the mind (consciousness) and with which it is organically connected, it's natural to guess that the above-mentioned feature of knowledge—its becoming a thing or its objectification in concepts—has an objective foundation and that consequently we can find in reality itself an analogous phenomenon or process. And in truth, if we look at those organic processes in which a certain potentiality gets actualized and gives rise to determinate vital forms, then, it seems, just there something is happening that is similar to the objectification of cognition in the consciousness, for the objectifying of concepts *eo ipso* means the actualizing of a certain potentiality.

On the other hand, ideal being is crystallized out of abstraction and reflection, i.e., two acts of thinking with which nothing in the organic world can be compared and which distinguish man from the rest of nature. By creating an ideal sphere of concepts these faculties of the conscious mind enable man to overcome the indeterminacy that lies in real being and stems either from the non-thingly nature of being itself, or from the continuity of time and space, or from the opennes of the horizon of the future (time). Having conquered the indeterminateness of becoming and thrown off the shackles of real time, cognition rises up into the sphere of changeless being and thereby acquires new, hitherto unacknowledged possibilities. Thus the fixing of the world of ideas (the objectification of cognition) is the foundation of human cultural creativity. Even here, however, the dynamical moment always has precedence over the static moment. Spreading out and pushing deeper cognition itself explodes the forms it has created and surges up towards a goal which always remains transcendent to it.

Endnotes

1. Kant analyzed the general conditions of the *possibility* of knowledge (and objects of knowledge). The fact that these conditions are realized in empirical knowledge and in the world of empirical phenomena is purely coincidental and therefore remains beyond the horizon of Kant's philosophical problematics. Similarly Hegel emphasized that only that which is general constitutes the world's substantial, essential being. Thus in fact Hegel's dialectics, even if it takes note of the concrete totality of phenomena, eschews the problem of facticity.
2. Now, after the discovery of the neutron and positron, electronic theory became more complicated.
3. It is interesting to note that one of the constants on which the newest theories of physics are based is the *velocity of light*, i.e. a purely empirical magnitude, about which one cannot be certain that further experiments will not show it to be variable.
4. Compare what has been said earlier about the motion of a material point.
5. Cf. Sesemann W. Die logischen Gesetze und das Sein. In *Eranus*, 1931, vol. 2, pp. 59–230.
6. Ibid., pp. 161–163.
7. It is only by basing themselves on the world's contemplative aspect that the natural scientists of our times have been able to *geometrize* physics, i.e., to turn theoretical physics into a certain kind of non-Euclidean geometry.

A REVIEW OF WOROBIOW'S BOOK ON ČIURLIONIS

Nikolaj Worobiow's German-language monograph on M. K. Čiurlionis[1] is one of those comparatively rare books that first of all arouse in us a desire to thank the author sincerely. It not only gives us much interesting and valuable information about Čiurlionis's life and work but also enables us to delve deeper into the secret of the world he has created and to give coherence to what we ourselves have experienced in delightedly viewing his works. That is why, I think, this book will not only be of interest to the lovers of true art abroad but will also encourage all those here, in Lithuania, who are fond of, and feel close, to Čiurlionis's paintings to take a fresh and more penetrating look at them and to appreciate even more carefully what this one-of-a-kind painter has given us. In this brief review I do not intend to cover everything that is interesting and noteworthy in Worobiow's monograph. I will content myself with bringing out those thoughts that are especially important for understanding Čiurlionis's creativity.

First of all the author persuasively shows that the evolution of Čiurlionis as an artist falls into three periods clearly different in style and technical skills. The *first*, *initial*, *period* encompasses the years when Čiurlionis, having turned away from music and devoted himself to painting, has not yet found the right optical form for his spiritual visions: he just flows with the symbolist (modernist) current that dominates the poetry and visual arts of those times. It is precisely the influence of literary subjects and ideas that makes itself felt in the allegorical character of Čiurlionis's first works. They seem to be illustrations for unwritten poems. The paintings are not yet self-sufficient; they depend on projects from another branch of art. Nor is the formal side of these paitings flawless. The color scale used is not well-balanced; it is marked by a certain graphical etchyness.

But even in this first period the main direction of Čiurlionis's art is already incipient. What primarily attracts and inspires him is nature itself, the riddle of its organic vitality, its mysterious connection with human nature and destiny—in a word, everything that appears in nature to an artist truly in love with it and capable of dedicating himself to its contemplation. His favorite subject is the mood-filled landscape. However, Čiurlionis's originality, which blossoms forth in the *second period* of his creativity, lies not in his choice of this subject—a direction shared by the progressive art of those times in Poland, Germany, and other countries—but in the way he conceives of it and with what stylistic means he treats this subject; finally, it lies in the way he clothes his universal visions in a national form. He paints Lithuanian nature and knows like no one else how to evoke its characteristic qualities and peculiar charm. His works at once display the boundlessness of the universe and a vitality that spiritualizes all. That's why Čiurlionis in his paintings most often chooses the spectator's viewpoint in such a way as to reveal to him the unlimited depth of light-suffused space. The means whereby he achieves this extraordinary effect—for example, in depicting the star-studded night sky or the breadth of the earth's horizon—are amazing in their simplicity and strict determinacy. On the one hand, there is the raising to a higher degree of the same color (e.g., green); on the other, we have the thinning stripes running toward the horizon (e.g., rivers) or rows of perspectively diminishing things (e.g., trees) leading the gaze into unreachable distances.

There is another thing important to Čiurlionis, and that's his aim to express the dynamism of nature's vitality. Thus he strives to overcome the static nature of painting by bringing it closer to other branches of art, in particular the one that was especially dear to him—music. He does not content himself with a single painting, but develops his chosen subject in a series of works that depict different stretches of the same process. In addition, even in an individual painting the composition is full of dynamism: its elements are rhythmically divided and grouped in such a way that they appear to be moving in a single sweep driven by the same elemental force. And note that all the parts are organically tied into a whole; not one of them stands out independently; and only in its connection with the others does each part acquire its true significance and painterly value. That's why even a human being has no exclusive place in Čiurlionis's works. He or she is only a creature of nature, along with the others; Čiurlionis never emphasizes a human being's independent individuality.

Finally, his mature painting is marked by one more conspicuous feature which Worobiow very aptly calls an "optic (visual) metaphor." The things Čiurlionis paints are simplified and at the same time dematerialized in such a way that their shapes merge with those of other things and thereby become ambiguous. That very same form, for example, can appear simultaneously as a star, blossom, flame, and snowflake. In this way Čiurlionis gives his paintings an extraordinary abundance of content and significance while staying within the boundaries of the possibilities available to painting.

The *third and final period* of Čiurlionis's creativity was conditioned by the time he spent in St. Petersburg. There he met and became friends with that period's most illustrious Russian painters who had gathered around the magazine *Mir iskusstva* (World of Art). Their extremely elegant way of painting impressed Čiurlionis deeply and encouraged him to perfect and enrich his technique. His works from this period take on a decorative nature and tend toward a certain graphicality. The composition is generally based

M. K. Čiurlionis. Sonata of the Pyramids. Scherzo. 1909

M. K. Čiurlionis National Art Museum
Photograph by Arūnas Baltėnas

on a strict geometric schema.² Direct intuition is subordinated to formal tasks. This doesn't mean that Čiurlionis's creative powers have declined. In dedicating himself to mastering form, he sought new ways of realizing his artistic projects. Only a premature, tragic death prevented this quest from coming to the anticipated fruition.

Especially interesting is the way Worobiow elucidates the relationship of painting and music in Čiurlionis's work. Beauty and artistry of sensory form was not a self-sufficient goal for him, only a means to express the way he saw, understood, and felt the world. Since its aural aspect was no less important to him than the visual, it is understandable why he was eager to draw them closer together by infusing painting with musical elements. Already the romanticists had dreamed about a synthesis of different branches of art. In Čiurlionis's time some visual artists attempted, by an abstract, ornamental manner of drawing, to go beyond the confines of theme painting and to obtain effects similar to those of music and lyric poetry. However, only Čiurlionis explicitly embodied the type *painter-musician*. Not in the sense that he conjoined or merged these distinct art branches by applying musical forms to painting, but in the sense that in his painting he called attention to, and emphasized, everything that has an affinity to music. It would be erroneous to suppose that in those series of paintings that are called sonatas the sonata form is truly recreated. With respect to their composition they are no different from those paintings to which Čiurlionis did not give musical names. But both types of painting are filled with a certain musical mood. What are these painterly means that allow this mood to assert itself so explicitly and impressively?

We already mentioned that Čiurlionis's art is characterized by dynamism and a rhythmical repetition of the same motifs variously appearing in diverse planes of spatial perspective. In order to emphasize this repetition and paralleling of motifs Čiurlionis likes to use reflections of objects on water surfaces. In this way the painting's whole structure comes to resemble a polyphonic orchestral composition where every instrument's voice responds to the voices of other instruments, all together forming a powerful harmonious chord. The melody (theme) corresponds to a broad sweep of line; tonality and modulations correspond to the general background color and its diverse variations. This musical impression is supported and strengthened by optical metaphors. The tendency of the individual forms to be multiply ambiguous in meaning weakens, to some extent, their thingly significance and does not allow one objective meaning to trump all the others. The dematerialization of thingly forms and colors pulls in the same direction. In these paintings Čiurlionis's colors are translucent and ethereally light. The shapes of things, simplified and schematized, also seem to lose their material mass and to turn into incorporeal dream images.

In a word, the whole visible world acquires a spiritualized appearance and thus moves closer to the world of musical sounds, since dematerialization enables colours and shapes to permeate each other and intermingle in the way that tones sounding together in an orchestra do.

Thus, in orienting himself to music, Čiurlionis doesn't bring anything to painting that would be alien to its nature. On the contrary, this orientation even helped him to impress upon his visible forms a stricter coherence and a more explicit unity.

On the other hand, Čiurlionis's music (as exemplified by the tone poems *In the Forest* and *The Sea*) possesses an extraordinary painterly quality deriving from the same source that informs his painting—his love of nature and his fascination with its hatmonies. Still, in Worobiow's view, the significance of music for Čiurlionis is somewhat different. In his last compositions the "nocturnal" (dark) side of his soul—the one that determined his tragic fate—clearly and unmitigatedly comes to the fore.

I hope that the fate of Worobiow's monograph is the one it deserves.

Endnotes

1 Nikolaj Worobiow, *M. K. Čiurlionis, der litausche Maler und Musiker*, Kaunas und Leipzig, 1938.
2 Worobiow correctly indicates that Čiurlionis's decorative style has some affinity to the paintings and graphic arts of the Far East.

Index

A
Anaxagoras, xi
Anaximander, xi
Antisthenes, xi
Aristotle, xi, xvi, 29
Augustine, Saint, xxi–xxii, xxvii, xxix

B
Bacon, Francis, xi
Bayer, Raymond, 31
Baumgarten, Alexander, 30
Beethoven, Ludwig van, 4, 6
Bergson, Henri, xx, xxiii–xxiv, xxvi, xxix, 61, 73
Boileau, Nicolas, 29
Botz-Bornstein, Thorsten, xii, xvi, xxxi
Broglie, Louis de, 65
Bruckner, Anton, 6
Buber, Martin, xix
Bülow, Hans von, 6

C, Č
Cassirer, Ernst, xv
Christiansen, Boder, 3, 5, 10, 15
Cohen, Hermann, xv
Comte, Auguste, xi
Croce, Benedetto, xi, 31
Čiurlionis, Mikalojus Konstantinas, xii–xiii, 46, 53, 81–82, 84–85

D
Descartes, René, 56
Dilthey, Wilhem, xvii, xvii
Dirac, Paul, 65
Drunga, Mykolas, xvi

E
Einstein, Albert, 67
Euclid, 63–64, 66

Epicurus, xi
Epictetus, xi

F
Fechner, Gustav Theodor, xi, 31
Feuerbach, Ludwig, xi
Fichte, Johann Gottlieb, xi, xvii
Focillon, Henri, 31

G
Gadamer, Hans-Georg, xix
Geiger, Moritz, 31
Goethe, Johann Wolfgang von, 14
Groos, Karl, 31
Grosse, Ernst, 27
Guyau, Jean Marie, xi

H
Hartmann, Eduard, xi
Hartmann, Nicolai, x–xi, viii–ix
Hegel, Georg Wilhelm Friedrich, xi, xx–xxi, 31, 60
Heidegger, Martin, xi, xvi–xvii, xx, xxii–xxiii–xxiv, xxv–xxvi, xxix, xxxi–xxxiii, 59
Heisenberg, Werner, 65
Helvetius, Claude Adrien, xi
Heraclitus, xi
Herbart, Johann Friedrich, 31
Herder, Johann Gottfried von, ix, xi
Hildebrandt, A.von, 31
Hobbes, Thomas, xi
Holbach, Paul, xi
Homer, 34–35
Hume, David, 30, 67
Husserl, Edmund, xi, xix, xxii, 55, 59
Hutcheson, Francis, 30

J
Jaques-Dalcroze, Émile, 36
Jaspers, Karl, xxvii–xxviii, 59, 88

K
Kant, Immanuel, ix, xx, xxiv, xxix, 7, 15, 30, 55–56, 63–64, 73, 79
Kierkegaard, Søren, xxix, xxxiii

L
Leibniz, Gottfried Wilhem, 30
Lenin, Vladimir, xxx
Lermontov, Mikhail, 7, 18
Lessing, Gotthold Ephraim, 17
Lévinas, Emmanuel, xix–xx, xxv–xxvi xxix–xxx, xxxi–xxxiii
Lipps, Theodor, xvii, 31
Lobachevsky, Nikolai, 63
Lossky, Nikolai, xv–xvi, 73
Lotze, Hermann, 31

M
Maxwell, J. C., 65

N
Natorp, Paul, xv
Nemeth, Thomas, xxxi
Nekrasov, Nikolai, 3
Nietzsche, Friedrich, xviii, xxi
Nikisch, Arthur, 6

P
Pfänder, Alexander, 59
Plato, 22, 29, 39–42, 60
Pushkin, Alexander, 3, 7, 12, 14, 18, 52

R
Raphael, 3
Rembrandt, Harmensz van Rijn, 3
Riemann, Bernhard, 63
Romano, Giulio, 3

S, Š
Šalkauskis, Stasys, x
Sartre, Jean-Paul, xix, xxx
Scheler, Max, xvii, 59
Schelling, Friedrich Wilhem, 15, 31
Schopenhauer, Arthur, 7, 31
Schrödinger, Erwin, 65
Sesemann, Vasily, ix–xxxiii
Shaftesbury, Lord, 30
Socrates, 33
Sverdiolas, Arūnas, ix, xiii, xv

T
Taine, Hippolyte, 3, 27
Tchaikovsky, Pyotr, 6
Tumelis, Juozas, xii

V
Velazquez, Diego Rodríguez de Silva y, 4
Volkelt, Johannes, 31

W
Winckelmann, Johann Joachim, 16
Wittgenstein, Ludwig, xvii
Wolff, Christian, 30
Wölfflin, Heinrich, xv, 19, 27, 31
Worobiow, Nikolaj, xii, 81–82, 84–85

Z
Zielinski, Tadeusz, xv

www.ingramcontent.com/pod-product-compliance
Lightning Source LLC
Chambersburg PA
CBHW070629300426
44113CB00010B/1710